The Critical Idiom

Founder Editor: John D. Jump (1969–1976)

44   Lyric

Lyric

David Lindley

Methuen
London and New York

First published in 1985 by
Methuen & Co. Ltd
11 New Fetter Lane,
London EC4P 4EE

Published in the USA by
Methuen & Co.
in association with Methuen, Inc.
29 West 35th Street,
New York, NY 10001

Typeset by
Scarborough Typesetting Services
and printed in Great Britain by
J. W. Arrowsmith (Bristol) Ltd

British Library
Cataloguing in Publication Data

Lindley, David
Lyric. – (The Critical idiom; 44)
1. Lyric poetry
I. Title.   II. Series
809.1'4   PN1356

ISBN 0–416–31430–9
ISBN 0–416–31440–6 Pbk

Library of Congress
Cataloging in Publication Data

Lindley, David, 1948–
Lyric.
(The Critical idiom; 44)
Bibliography: p.
Includes index.
1. English poetry – History and
criticism. 2. Lyric poetry – History
and criticism.
I. Title.   II. Series
PR509.L8L56   1985
821'.04'09   85–4891

ISBN 0–416–31430–9
ISBN 0–416–31440–6 (pbk.)

61

For Steve and Stuart,
Les, Malcolm and Nicholas

Contents

Acknowledgements

The author and publisher gratefully acknowledge permission to reproduce the following copyright material in this book:

W. H. Auden, for lines from 'Anthem for St. Cecilia's Day' from *Collected Poems*, ed. Edward Mendelson, copyright 1976 by the Estate of W. H. Auden. Reprinted by permission of Faber and Faber and Random House, Inc.

Noel Coward, 'Mad Dogs and Englishmen', published by Methuen. Reprinted by permission of the Estate of Noel Coward.

Gavin Ewart, for lines from 'They flee from me' from *The New Ewart*, reprinted by permission of Hutchinson Publishing Group Limited.

John Fuller, for lines from 'Valentine' from *The Beautiful Inventions*. Reprinted by permission of Martin Secker and Warburg Ltd.

Seamus Heaney, for line from 'Glanmore Sonnets X' from *Field Work*, copyright 1976, 1979 by Seamus Heaney. Reprinted by permission of Faber and Faber Limited and Farrar, Straus and Giroux, Inc.

Geoffrey Hill, for the twelfth lyric from 'Pentecost Castle' from *Tenebrae* (1978). Reprinted by permission of Andre Deutsch.

Linton Kwesi Johnson, for 'Reggae Sounds' from *Dread Beat and Blood*. Reprinted by permission of Bogle-L'Ouverture Publications Ltd.

Denise Levertov, for lines from 'A Common Ground' from *Poems 1960–1967*. Copyright 1961 by Denise Levertov Goodman.

Preface

Unlike many of the books in this series, this study confines itself almost entirely to poetry written in English. While sensible of the great losses this entails, and the potential distortions that result from ignoring the poetry of other languages, it seemed that, with such a large terrain, some limitation of scope was essential.

In the discussion that follows I am only too well aware of the gaps and simplifications that compression necessitates and ignorance engenders. Many colleagues in the School of English have patiently endured inquisition, and by their generous offering of information and suggestion have attempted to save me from error. My thanks go to Professor John Barnard, David Fairer, Lesley Johnson, Susan Matthews, Alastair Stead and John Whale. So too, the students in my post-graduate class helped enormously to clarify the nature of the problems that defining the lyric entails, and my gratitude is recorded in the dedication. Ruth and Liz Neat initiated me into the *terra incognita* of 'pop' lyric, and to them, and the many other individuals who have over the years extended my poetic horizons, I acknowledge my debt.

My thanks also go to Angela Archdale, Debbie Brown and Doreen Pine for their typing of the manuscript.

1
Categories and definitions

The term 'lyric' is, in critical vocabulary, particularly elusive of definition. It has at various times been employed to perform a number of discriminatory tasks, but the levels of its meaning and usefulness have not usually been distinguished coherently and consistently. It has been pressed into service as a *universal*, co-operating with 'epic' and 'drama' in the carving up of literature's empire. It has served as a more specific label for one among many poetic *genres*. From conflation of these two functions have come many of the contradictions that muddy the implication of the adjective 'lyrical' when used as a *modal* term applied to parts of non-lyric poems, to novels or films. The purpose of this opening chapter is to attempt to clarify these different uses of the term.

I

For critics in all periods the etymological derivation of 'lyric' from the lyre has furnished one element of the definition of lyric as universal. But whereas for the Greeks it made sense to distinguish 'lyric' (sung) from 'epic' (recited) and 'drama' (spoken), a necessary connection of lyric poetry with accompanying music was broken early, and a social reality slipped into metaphor. When Horace called poems *Carmina* he gestured towards a tradition of song, but did not describe his own practice. In subsequent generations attempts to isolate the 'music' of poetry, whether by Pater, Pound, Eliot or Frye (to name but a few), have been searches for one of the fundamental possibilities that poetic utterance may tap, describing a universal, not a genre. None the less, the poem written to be sung remains the one kind to which no critic can deny the label 'lyric', and the implications of this musical relationship will be further investigated in Chapter 2.

The categorization of lyric as 'poetry that sings' has been very influential, often made to stand in opposition to 'poetry of speech', but is only one defining constituent in the three-way slicing of the literary cake into epic, dramatic and lyric which became a fixed feature of descriptive and prescriptive practice in later periods, reaching its height in the nineteenth century, and still reverberating in our own time. Many ingenious analogies have been used to define and support the notion of a literary trinity, and the reader who wishes to investigate them should consult the works by Heather Dubrow, Paul Hernadi and René Wellek listed in the bibliography, for, interesting though they may be for the history of aesthetic theory, they must lie outside the scope of this study.

There are, however, three qualities that have fairly consistently been attached to the idea of lyric as a universal category, and since they underlie many of the casual uses of the term in critical writing, they need further discussion.

In the first place 'lyric' is held to apply to poems employing a first-person speaker, and, by extension, to indicate a preoccupation with the expression of individual feeling or emotion. The distinction between a poet speaking in his own voice or speaking through a character was made by Plato, but a close connection of lyric with a first-person speaker was most firmly established by German writers of the Romantic period, and became standard in nineteenth-century England, when Ruskin defined lyric poetry as 'the expression by a poet of his own feelings'. In more recent times the subjectivity of lyric is an assumption underlying Kate Hamburger's dualistic schema, and is a constituent of the 'lyrical principle' elaborated by Emil Staiger. It is duly embalmed in most dictionary definitions of lyric.

The problematic nature of the identification of lyric with first-person poems is obvious. Though it is one of the devices that poets may employ, it is by no means self-evident that all poetry using this mode of speech is 'lyric', nor that poetry which does not should be excluded from the lyric category. Ballads are designed for singing but are frequently narrative and communal rather than personal; many twentieth-century lyric poets have striven to efface the poet from the poem.

The second commonly accepted attribute of the lyric is that it deals in the present tense, with the immediacy of felt experience. It is this aspect that Barbara Hardy highlights in her study *The Advantage of Lyric*, and which Jonathan Culler explores in his essay 'Apostrophe' in *The Pursuit of Signs*. Culler's argument is that the rhetorical tactic of apostrophe moves the lyric poem from enslavement to temporal narrative, freeing it for the celebration of 'the *now* of discourse, of writing'. He suggests 'that one distinguish two forces in poetry, the narrative and the apostrophic, and that the lyric is characteristically the triumph of the apostrophic' (p. 149).

There can be no doubt that lyrics frequently do concentrate on single moments of heightened awareness or feeling, but thus to circumscribe the lyric would exclude many poems that are unambiguously narrative, and furthermore runs the risk of simplifying the struggle that many lyrics enact. Sharon Cameron concludes her study of *Lyric Time* (devoted chiefly, but not exclusively, to Emily Dickinson) thus:

> The deathless world of no time is a world we lose by merely waking up. Dickinson's poems articulate the loss, and, like all lyrics, they attempt to reverse it. If she dreamed this reversal bolder than most lyrics do, throwing into relief the shape of the lyric struggle itself, she also knew more profoundly the shocking certainty of its disappointment.
>
> (p. 260)

One other adjective appears in most dictionary definitions – 'short'. Eliot exasperatedly enquired 'how short does a poem have to be, to be called a lyric?' (*On Poetry and Poets*, London, 1957, p. 97).

He speaks for the obvious point that a term so vague cannot apparently be useful. Yet, in purely pragmatic terms, brevity is probably the one quality that most people would agree upon when compiling anthologies of 'lyrics'.

But it is clear that no attempt to arrive at a description of the lyric as a universal can ever quite succeed. Though one might not agree with Wellek that 'nothing beyond generalities of the tritest kind can result from it' (*Discriminations*, p. 252), since speculation on what Goethe called the *Naturformen der Dichtung* has its place in a general aesthetics, it must be acknowledged, as Guillèn asserts, 'that these essential modes or universals do not coincide with the historically determined, practically oriented, form-conscious categories that one might call genres' (*Literature as System*, Princeton, 1971, pp. 114–15). E. D. Hirsch's sensible words about the concept of 'literature' can appropriately be transferred to discussion of 'lyric':

> We get into trouble when we assume that the classification really *has* a boundary line or means the same thing in different uses. The only embarrassment to be suffered from the amorphousness of words is the attempt to pretend that they are not amorphous. Literary theory gets into trouble only when it pretends that the word *literature* can be satisfactorily defined, and then tries to erect generalisations on such a delusive definition.
>
> ('What Isn't Literature', in *What is Literature?*, ed. Paul Hernadi, Bloomington and London, 1978, p. 26)

We may then accept that many lyrics are short, many speak of heightened feeling in a poetic present and are uttered by a voice in the first person, and a significant number are written for music or out of a musical impulse. But many other poems we might wish to call 'lyrics' have few or none of these qualities, and in order to sharpen the applications of the term it is towards its use as generic description that we must turn.

II

One way out of the problems that beset the word is to use it as an umbrella covering a variety of generic subclasses. Paul Hernadi in *Beyond Genre* represents the territory of the lyric diagrammatically, moving between 'meditative poetry' and 'quasi-dramatic monologue' on one axis, 'songlike poems' and 'objective correlative' on the other. J. W. Jackson in the *Princeton Encyclopaedia of Poetry and Poetics* (ed. Alex Preminger, Princeton, 1974) divides it into 'the lyric of vision or emblem', 'the lyric of thought or idea' and 'the lyric of emotion or feeling'. Both these attempts are interesting and it is certainly necessary to subdivide the genres of lyric, but each of them struggles with the fact that the notion poets and readers have of lyric genres is profoundly affected by fluctuation in systems of classification and poetic practice through history. For it is the recognition of historical variation that characterizes the difference between assertions about the lyric as a universal and the pursuit of a clearer understanding of the lyric as genre. The universalist wishes to make statements that will be true for all time and measures individual examples against an inflexible standard. The generic critic recognizes change.

It is obviously impossible in a study of this length to attempt a potted history of the European, or even of the English lyric. What follows is a selective isolation of some major issues.

In classical Greek, 'lyric' is a precise generic delineation, distinguished not only from 'epic' and 'drama', but from other poetic genres, such as 'elegy' (originally sung to the flute rather than the lyre). It could, however, be subdivided even then into the choral songs of Pindar and the solo songs of Sappho and Anacreon. Each of these divisions corresponds more or less exactly with formal differences – the triadically arranged elaborate strophes of Pindar against the simpler repeated stanza forms of Sappho or Alcaeus. The content, too, can be distinguished – the public praise of heroes in Pindar from the love songs or drinking songs of Sappho or Anacreon. All these lyrics had specific social functions. In them the consorting of form, content and mode of presentation gives a secure generic identity.

This very simplified version of Greek lyric is the one which transmitted itself to the Renaissance, as Drayton's preface to his *Odes* indicates:

> an Ode is knowne to have been properly a Song, modulated to the ancient Harpe, and neither too short-breathed, as hasting to the end, nor composed of the longest Verses. . . . They are (as the Learned say) divers: Some transcendently loftie, and farre more high then the Epick . . . witnesse those of the inimitable *Pindarus*, consecrated to the glorie and renowne of such as returned in triumph from *Olympus*. . . . Others, among the Greekes, are amorous, soft and made for Chambers, as other for Theaters; as were *Anacreon's* . . . of a mixed kinde were Horaces.

This statement has a number of interesting implications. First, Drayton accepts an hierarchic system of generic classification which runs from lofty poetry in praise of gods and princes down to that for recreation. The lyric straddles that hierarchy, appearing at both top and bottom. The range of possible subject-matter is a perennial problem in the description of lyric genres, and in no insignificant measure the history of the lyric has been one of movement down and up the hierarchy of literary kinds. For Drayton it is the musical connection that holds together this disparate matter in a single genre. But for him Greek practice was mediated through Roman writers, and, as for Horace, the linking of lyric to music was more a question of adopting certain formal models, appropriate versification and conventional gestures to the 'lyre' than of anticipating actual musical setting. (The sense of lyric's musical origin does, however, enable him to smuggle into his collection a ballad, 'Fair stood the wind for France'. Its praise of Henry V is elevated to the status of an ode because of its analogy with Pindaric musical praise of heroes.) Drayton also shows himself aware of the importance of social function in defining genre. The word 'chambers' accommodates classical practice to the contemporary courtly world of the 'game of love', permitting his *Odes* to mix together motifs derived from classical poets with those descended from more recent Petrarchan tradition in a characteristic manoeuvre for extending a genre's allowable subject-matter.

Drayton, then, has a fairly clear notion of the lyric genre as being defined by function, form and subject-matter (significantly without any mention of personal voice or feeling), though the strains within so wide-ranging a genre held together by the notional cement of a musical original are also clearly implicit.

His classification is hierarchic. Equally significant was the 'horizontal' division of lyric into sacred and secular (Feste's 'love song, or song of good life'). Though sacred subjects are *de facto* more 'serious' than secular, in the Middle Ages there was free interchange between them. A lack of embarrassment in translating ordinary life into a religious dimension gives a wonderful intimacy to poems about the Virgin Mary rocking her child, or about Mary as mankind's lover, as it accounts for the ease with which learned biblical typology is incorporated into the apparent simplicity of a lyric like 'I sing of a maiden that is makeless'. Conversely, praises of a mistress are made more fervent by the free adoption of quasi-religious terminology.

In the Renaissance, a poet like Donne could still use the resonances of religious vocabulary to praise his mistress or like Herbert could invest everyday reality with religious significance, but there is during the period rather more separation of kinds. Herrick's *Hesperides* are answered by *Noble Numbers*; Campion's 'Divine and Morall Songs' published alongside 'Light Conceits of Lovers' in *Two Bookes of Ayres*. The religious lyric develops its own taxonomy, derived from the fusion of a classical generic system with one derived from the Scriptures, as Barbara Lewalski describes:

We find, in general, three chief kinds of biblical lyrics identified on the basis of the Pauline texts. The first kind are prayer-like or meditative poems called psalms, evidently lending themselves to self-probing and petitionary postures. The second are hymns – praises of and thanksgivings to God in a particularly sublime and exalted style; this generic conception is in line with the classical and neo-classical location of the hymn to the gods at the apex of the epideictic kinds. . . . The third kind are 'spiritual songs', evidently artful, elegant, ode-like poems celebrating special occasions and lofty matters.

(Protestant Poetics, p. 39)

Sacred and secular lyrics are, then, generic twins, similar but distinct kinds. They continue to affect one another. (For example, the tradition of affective devotion stretching back to the Middle Ages which required intense concentration on biblical scenes and application of that meditation to the personal life of the poet may, as Louis L. Martz argues in *The Poetry of Meditation* (New Haven and London, 1954) and in *The Poem of the Mind* (New York, 1966), have had considerable effect upon the practice of secular poetry from the Renaissance to the present day.) It is important to recognize not only the high spots in the history of the religious lyric – Herbert or Hopkins for example, but also the continuing tradition of hymnody that is simple but not unserious, public by function and use as little literary secular lyric is, and that retains a clear and unembarrassed didactic aim. It is a tradition that, despite the efforts of a few critics, notably Donald Davie (in *Purity of Diction in English Poetry*), is generally peripheral to literary study. It deserves greater attention, for its intrinsic merit and because of the particular use that poets like Blake, Emily Dickinson or Stevie Smith make of it, and especially, in the context of the present discussion, for the importance it has had for generations of ordinary readers in conditioning their understanding of what constitutes lyric poetry.

So far, sheltering under the lyric umbrella we have found subjects high and low, sacred and secular. To find other vantage points from which to define lyric it is useful to consider its relationships with poetic genres that lie upon its borders. It is an obvious tactic to define a term by demonstrating what it is not. But the history of the lyric is more difficult than that, for at various times it has been affected by its near neighbours in significant ways, so that the pursuit of clarity must also take on board the fact of confusion.

Three examples only must serve as illustrations. The first concerns lyric's briefer neighbour, the epigram. Brevity and pointedness are essential to epigram, and generally it is assumed that its characteristic tone will be sharp and satirical. Furthermore, as Barbara H. Smith observes in her acute comments on the epigram:

> To 'dispel' (to undo the spell) or to dismiss is the epigrammatist's characteristic gesture. In love or hate, praise or blame, he is saying something so that he will not have to say it again. He writes a poem not when he is moved, but when he ceases to be. He records the moment of mastery – not the emotion, but the attitude that conquered it.
>
> (*Poetic Closure*, p. 208)

In this respect epigram seems antithetic to lyric. But during the Renaissance, as Alastair Fowler in *Kinds of Literature* and Rosalie Colie in *The Resources of Kind* have demonstrated, the epigrammatic mode had considerable effect upon lyric poetry, especially upon the sonnet. In part this is attributable to the rediscovery of the manuscripts of *The Greek Anthology*, which contained epigrams of love, tempering the assumptions of epigram's bitterness. But at the same time the epigrammatic modulation of lyric occurred precisely because it offered something that poets were disposed to use – a way of transforming the repetitive and paratactic structures characteristic of song lyric in the direction of wit and logical development. Furthermore it sanctioned the sometimes bitter and cynical tone of Donne and the Cavalier lyricists, assisting their assault upon conventions of love poetry.

The fact of the influence of epigram upon lyric also tells us something of the way poets at the time thought of the lyric genre itself. The artifice of an aristocratic, courtly poetry encourages detachment and irony at the expense of the poet–speaker. Sidney's *Astrophil and Stella* exploits the play between traditional love-longing and epigrammatic irony to telling effect; many of Donne's lyrics depend upon a sudden turn which jolts the reader out of his immersion in a lyric world of feeling. Ben Jonson's moving poem 'On My First Son', in contrast, marks the achievement of resignation to loss by a modulation from lyric to epigrammatic tellingly achieved as the voice of the poet–speaker gives way to words spoken from the tomb of his dead son. (The control of this poem can profitably be compared with that achieved in Jon Silkin's much more nakedly lyric poem 'Death of a Son' by understatement and poignant imagery.)

The epigrammatic lyric, extremely common in the Renaissance, did not, of course, disappear. The solidity of epigrammatic closure, the economy of its means, and the detachment it allows are still qualities which poets can make use of and set in fruitful relationship with more fluid form and introspective stance. William H. Pritchard's description of contemporary poetry as manifesting 'the lyric impulse to soar in contention and cooperation with a wryly satiric and earthbound one' (Reuben A. Brower (ed.), *Forms of Lyric*, p. 150) testifies to its exploitation in our own time.

Epigram pulls lyric one way; the second neighbouring kind to be considered takes it in a different direction. Elegy in classical literature, functionally differentiated by its flute accompaniment, came to be distinguished from other kinds by its metre, the elegiac distich of hexameter and pentameter. But, as Fowler observes, the elegy 'was not a blank, subject-free, purely formal genre. Even in its extensions it retained the character of passionate meditation' (*Kinds of Literature*, p. 136).

In the Renaissance there were two kinds of elegy, the love elegy and the elegy of commemoration. The love elegy, modelled on

Latin poetry, especially Ovid's *Amores*, was distinguished from lyric partly on metrical grounds. Donne's *Songs and Sonets* are in stanza forms, where the *Elegies* are in couplets. This more open form permitted an expansive meditation on topics of love, and greater scope for narrative than the tighter confines of lyric. Where epigram pushes the lyric towards compression, elegy opens it, among other things, to quasi-personal 'passionate meditation'. The co-presence of these neighbours leads Fowler to produce a somewhat Polonian description of 'the witty, pointed love elegy that we know as Metaphysical lyric' (p. 222). Yet the lyric remains a distinct genre, poised between the kinds of 'sweet' epigram and love elegy. Campion's 'It fell on a somer's day', for example, is both a compression of an Ovidian narrative elegy and at the same time an amplification of two of his own Latin epigrams.

The commemorative elegy developed its own repertory of subject-matter and structure more clearly than the love elegy. It customarily included praise of the departed and lament at the cruelty of fate, and ended with consolation. These topoi, however, might appear within the brief compass of epitaph or epigram, be cast in stanzaic lyric form, or else be expressed in ampler continuous metres. (All three can be found in Ben Jonson's work.)

In the subsequent history of elegy, the formal constraint disappears. As Wellek and Warren comment, 'Gray's "Elegy", written in the heroic quatrain, not in couplets, effectually destroys any continuation in English of elegy as any tender personal poem written in end-stopped couplets' (*Theory of Literature*, pp. 231–2). Gray's poem also marks the extension of elegy's subject-matter to melancholy meditation upon loss, an extension which squeezes out from the generic repertory the love elegy as it exists in Ovid, Donne or Carew.

This loosening of the boundaries of elegy has further consequence. M. H. Abrams, in *The Mirror and the Lamp*, traces the way concentration upon feeling and expressiveness means that, during the eighteenth and nineteenth centuries, the lyric poem becomes a 'poetic norm', a 'paradigm for poetic theory'. Alastair Fowler sees the interiorization of ode and other lyric kinds as exemplifying a modulation of lyric by elegy. He describes elegy as 'passionate meditation', leading to 'recognition (*anagnorosis*) of feeling, to revelations and illuminations' (*Kinds of Literature*, p. 207). If elegy is thus understood, then indeed it may be seen as dominant in English poetry from the Romantics to Hardy.

The net effect of the blurring of boundaries between elegy and lyric is to redraw the generic map. 'Elegy' as a distinct genre retreats to poetry in commemoration of the dead, while passionate, personal meditation becomes a defining quality of poems that would call themselves lyrics. (In the process, however, we are left without a name for longer meditative poems, particularly those in continuous metres.)

A further consequence of this shift in the understanding of lyric was to give much greater significance to the differentiation of lyric and dramatic. Browning printed this 'Advertisement' at the beginning of his *Bells and Pomegranates*, No. III (1842): 'Such Poems as the following come properly enough, I suppose, under the head of "Dramatic Pieces", being, though for the most part Lyric in expression, always Dramatic in principle, and so many utterances of so many imaginary persons, not mine.'

In more recent times it has been the blurring of this once decisive boundary that has been of great significance for the nature of lyric. The search for a way out of Romantic subjectiveness took Pound and Eliot many ways, but among their sources was Browning, often taken to be the initiator of the dramatic monologue (but see Alan Sinfield's book, *Dramatic Monologue* (London, 1977) in this series). 'The Love Song of J. Alfred Prufrock' is a dramatic monologue and also, explicitly in its title, and implicitly in its employment of quasi-refrain and in its diction and rhythms, a lyric poem. The adoption of personae in modernist lyric is, as has often enough been remarked, symptomatic of twentieth-century anxieties about self-identity, and marks a deliberate effort to establish a new aesthetic. It is only one among many strategies that have diversified the lyric genres in this century, but the freedom it offers for a poet to accommodate voices not his own in lyric poems has been widely accepted.

These examples of interplay between lyric and other genres illustrate three major points. First, the openness of lyric to modulation by neighbouring kinds witnesses to the essentially protean character of the genre (and therefore to the problematic nature of the present enterprise). It is inevitable that a kind which has from its very beginnings embraced a wide variety of subject-matter and form, and for which the connection with music has, at least since Roman times, ceased to be the cement that binds the variety together, should be amenable to the different demands that successive generations of poets have made upon it.

But, secondly, the fact that such modulations can be felt and described, the fact that epigram, elegy and dramatic monologue remain distinguishable genres, implies that there is some centre that accepts such modulation.

Thirdly, however, it has to be recognized that the successive modulations of lyric themselves modify the perception of the lyric centre. Further complication then ensues, since no lyric state is completely lost, and poets seeking to escape from the preferred conventions of their present may look back to the past. Eliot's resurrection of Donne is a celebrated example. Even then, we must acknowledge that poets perceive the past in ways coloured by prevailing notions of the lyric genre. So, for example, Pindar for Ben Jonson was primarily a formal model; for Cowley, Shelley or Robert Duncan (in his 'A Poem beginning with a line by Pindar'), his ghost performs quite different functions in defining the nature of their lyric enterprise.

In this sea of variables it might seem that all hope of circumscribing lyric genres must perish. Yet awareness of historical variation at the very least prevents the misreadings that come from approaching the literature of the past with inappropriate generic assumptions (of the kind, for example, that still lead undergraduates to worry about Donne's 'sincerity', or to bemoan the 'artificiality' of Sidney).

In approaching the poetry of our own time, when it is conventional to assert that the label 'lyric' is made to embrace material of such diversity that it is valueless, it is possible, with a historically sharpened generic sense, to see how competing schools may be distinguished by their attempts to pursue some, but not all, of the historical possibilities that lyric has entertained. So, for example, poets like Richard Wilbur or Philip Larkin distinguish their work by its disciplined use of stanza forms; the so-called 'confessional' poets seek to extend the ways in which lyric poetry may express the speaking self of the poet; beat poets, 'dub' poets and others attempt to reassert the musical connection of lyric.

III

'Genre should be conceived', write Wellek and Warren, 'as a grouping of literary works based, theoretically, upon both outer form (specific metre or structure) and also upon inner form (attitude, tone, purpose – more crudely, subject and audience)' (*Theory of Literature*, p. 231). Not the least of the problems in describing the lyric as a genre or cluster of genres is precisely that customary matches of external form with subject-matter and manner of presentation are extremely elusive.

One might begin by accepting the distinction Drayton makes between the greater and lesser lyric kinds. It was a basic categorization that persisted throughout the eighteenth century. In classical theory, and in later neo-classicism, the greater ode was marked off by its subject-matter (gods and heroes), by its form (the elaborate stanza forms of Pindar, mistakenly believed to be irregular) and by a characteristic style, 'falling from one thing into another after an Enthusiasticall manner' as Cowley describes it. Norman MacLean has traced the way in which, during the eighteenth century, the criteria of subject-matter and the epideictic character of the ode (as a rhetorical set-piece of praise or blame) give place to emphasis upon its sublimity, and thence to its presentation of the flights of poetic imagination ('From action to image', in *Critics and Criticism*, ed. R. S. Crane). As a consequence the distinction between greater and lesser kinds becomes much less clearly defined. As MacLean observes:

> The principles which had long served to divide poetry into kinds and to arrange them in a hierarchy, extending from epic and tragedy down to epigram (which could not always be distinguished from the lesser lyric) were not first principles to the Romantics. By the principles fundamental to the Romantics, poetry in the highest sense was one as the soul is; it was constituted, as is the soul, of the elements of thought and feeling; if divisible into important kinds, it was divisible by some such system as Wordsworth used in arranging his poems according to the psychological faculty predominant in the composition of each.
>
> (p. 459)

But though the hierarchic ranking of greater and lesser lyrics is significantly and permanently ruptured during this period, it does not follow that all of the distinctions perish. Poems entitled 'Ode' continue to be written. Though many are after the urbane Horatian model, rather than the enraptured Pindaric (from Pope's 'Ode to Solitude' or Collins's 'Ode to Evening' to Auden's 'Ode to the Medieval Poets'), irregular stanza forms attached to weighty subject-matter are an important generic signal for Wordsworth, Coleridge and Keats, as they are for Tennyson's 'Ode on the Death of The Duke of Wellington' or Allen Tate's 'Ode on the Confederate Dead'.

It is true, as John Jump observes in *The Ode* (London, 1974) in this series, that during the later nineteenth and twentieth centuries poets do not readily use the title 'Ode', and tend, if they do, to revert to its assocation with public poetry, or occasional subject, or at least apostrophic address. But the metrical freedom of Pindaric, associated with rapid movement of idea and image in poems usually of some length, and frequently implying some sense of the poet as *vates*, persists as an important dimension of lyric poetry.

Whitman (whom Swinburne celebrated as a 'strong-winged sou
with prophetic / Lips hot with the bloodbeats of song') belong
here, as does Hopkins. So too, one might argue, does the Pound o
the Cantos, and, in more recent times, the rhapsodies of Aller
Ginsberg or of Robert Duncan may be seen as exemplars of tha
same impulse, howsoever transformed.

Classification of the 'lesser' lyric kinds is even more problematic. In the classical period, as Horace's *Ars Poetica* makes clear
metrical distinctions were crucial to the delimitation of genres. I
is still true that a sense of lyrics as being poems in stanza form,
distinguishable from poems in more continuous metres, has some
generic force. Even practitioners of free verse often group the
words on the page so that they remind the reader of more fully
marked patterns from the past.

Choice of a particular metrical form may be significant in a
general way as a polemic gesture. Horace's adaptations of Greek
lyric metres to Latin verse signalled his effort to naturalize a
species of poetry out of favour in his society. Experiments with
quantitative metres in Europe in the sixteenth century were part of
the age's self-conscious classicism. They were usually linked with
attempts to recapture the effects of the fusion of music and words
in lyric poetry, and to dignify the genre by elevating it above the
'eare-pleasing rhymes without art' of ordinary song lyrics. (The
effort produced in English only a handful of poems that stand the
test of time — Campion's 'Rose-cheek't Laura' among them. The
seriousness of the attempt, as well as recognition of its inevitable
failure in English, can be seen in Jonson's 'A Fit of Rime against
Rime'.) Wordsworth's use of popular-ballad metre was a conscious
gesture in his project of returning poetic language to customary
speech. In our own time the adoption of any regular stanzaic form
tends to be an assertion of differentiation from those who employ
free verse. It indicates a refusal to surrender the artifice of poetry,
and frequently signals a desire to preserve or to reanimate tra-
ditions that a poet or group wishes to hold against the prevailing
wind.

Choice of particular fixed forms may, of course, tend to donate a characteristic quality to the poems they shape and therefore to condition the nature of the reading they demand. But with two major exceptions – the ballad stanza and the sonnet – fixed stanza forms tend not, of themselves, to predicate any particular subject-matter. The ballad stanza has a continuous history as a vehicle for narrative whether serious or comic. While it has been put to a wide variety of uses it tends always to suggest popular culture undistorted by false literariness, and to give the reader an illusion of a direct, unsophisticated address to primal situations and feelings. Wordsworth, Kipling and Charles Causley have all, in their very different ways, exploited these possibilities.

The stanza is also firmly associated with hymnody. (It is the double resonance of the form in both sacred and secular realms that perhaps helps it to accommodate subject-matter of a meditative kind.) The bitter power of Blake's ironies in the *Songs of Innocence and Experience* derives in no small measure from the way the metrical form prompts memories of conventional pieties against which his indictments are pitted. The reading of Emily Dickinson's brief meditations is deeply affected by their enigmatic play with the certainties that the faint presence of hymn measures suggests.

The sonnet form has, of course, been put to many uses, as John Fuller notes in *The Sonnet* in this series, and its canonic fourteen-line form has been extended or abbreviated, its rhyme schemes adapted or dispensed with. None the less the sonnet form has a repertoire of themes that poets may employ and depart from with some confidence that their readers will recognize the nature of the game.

The love sonnet, descended from Petrarch and institutionalized in English by the dominating presences of Sidney and Shakespeare, lies behind Meredith's ironic study of failing marriage in the extended sonnets of *Modern Love*, and serves as a point of departure for *Berryman's Sonnets*. The religious sonnets of Donne and Herbert are among the influences on Hopkins's works in the form;

Seamus Heaney's (unrhymed) 'Glanmore Sonnets' gesture towards the nature sonnets of the early nineteenth century; Lowell's *Notebook*, as Fuller suggests, mixes public and private themes in a fashion that owes something to Milton's extensions of the sonnet's range and seriousness.

Paul Fussell in *Poetic Meter and Poetic Form* and John Hollander in his entertaining *Rhyme's Reason* suggest other possible generic signals associated with particular stanza forms, but in the main a taxonomy of lyric poetry upon metrical grounds has limited possibility.

Classification by subject-matter poses problems of a rather different kind. In earlier periods a limited range of subjects might permit fairly large-scale divisions. Horace's categories of poems in praise of gods or men, love songs and drinking songs, or the troubadour classification of *canso* (love-song) and *sirventes* (public or moral subjects), have some usefulness in their own periods, but the continuous extension of the lyric repertoire means that such groupings proliferate. While love and death remain permanent lyric topics, and contemplation of external nature assumes its place in the generic repertory during the eighteenth century, the determination of Victorian and modern poets to admit no boundary to permissible topics, taken together with the shift already described from subject to quality of meditation as the determinant of lyric, mean that such large classes are not of much relevance to the experience of reading more recent poetry. But, paradoxically, as Fowler observes, 'In modern poetry, the collapse of many kinds into "lyric" has given subgenre an enlarged function' (*Kinds of Literature*, p. 114). These subgenres are defined almost entirely in terms of subject-matter.

It is, of course, the case that topics defined by subject-matter are not necessarily the same thing as 'genre' in the fuller sense, but, for all the problems, it is true that, as readers, we do associate lyrics by subject-matter, and that poets use conventional topoi as starting points for their lyric explorations.

Francis Cairns's book *Generic Composition in Greek and Roman Poetry* lists a wide variety of conventional subjects, and whether or

ot one accepts all the implications of his method it is very useful
for students of later poetry, and for the consideration of the classification of subgenres.

Some of the topoi he illustrates surface in English poetry. The
combination of 'threat prophecy' and 'gloating over fulfilment',
for example, appears frequently in Elizabethan love sonnets; the
propemtikon has a continued life in numerous Renaissance valedic-
tion poems. The *komos*, or appeal of the locked-out lover, finds its
way from Greek, through Latin, to songs such as Campion's
'Sweet, exclude me not' or (surprisingly enough) Bob Dylan's
'Temporary like Achilles'.

These continuities support Cairns's contention that 'all genres
originate in important, recurrent, real-life situations'. But the
vestigial survival of the motif of the excluded lover compared with
the frequency of persuasions to love in the sixteenth century and
beyond or the popularity of the post-coital poem in the twentieth
century makes an obvious point. As societies change, so do the
situations that lyric poetry may be called upon to represent. None
the less, a given convention of representation tends to fix, even
fossilize, certain kinds of experience as possible subject-matter (as
Gombrich tellingly demonstrates to be the case in the demesne of
the visual arts in his *Art and Illusion* (3rd edn, London, 1968)).

So, for example, the epithalamium or marriage song has a continuous history from the classical period to the present day. But
the ingredients which are included in any single example have
been variously determined by the survival (or archaeological
resuscitation) of details from Roman marriage rites, by the pressure of model texts by Catullus, Spenser and the Biblical *Song of
Songs*, as well as by a contemporary social reality. Similarly, a late-
medieval genre like the *aubade*, expressing the lover's regret at the
approach of day, has a continuous (and geographically wide-
spread) existence because it draws upon a universal experience.
But the shape it takes and the use to which it is put vary greatly.
Tenderness is a note sounded throughout its history, up to Patric
Dickinson's 'Aubade' in *A Rift in Time*. But the genre also

includes the fierce, triumphant wit of Donne's 'Busy old fool'; Empson's tersely circumstantial account of being wakened by an earthquake in his 'Aubade', and Lowell's bitter inversion of convention in 'Man and Wife', which records the failure of a marriage as 'the rising sun in war paint dyes us red'.

The medieval *chanson d'aventure* has an equally fruitful history. Its formulaic opening, 'As I walked out . . .' is usually the prelude to a meeting with a maiden. It persists in the broadside ballad and popular song (usually leading to an encounter anything but *courtois*), down to the 'punk poet' John Cooper Clarke's parody in 'salome maloney', which begins in time-honoured fashion: 'I was walking down oxford road'. Auden signals his intention to test conventional expectations when he opens his *chanson d'aventure* late in the day. 'As I walked out one evening' turns into a meditation upon time's destruction of love in a fruitful marrying of conventional topoi.

This formulaic opening was also frequently used in a religious context, often as a prelude to an encounter with the Virgin Mary and her child. One particularly fine variant, 'In the vaile of restles mynd' (discussed more fully on p. 54–5 below), leads to a meeting with the wounded Christ. It is this possibility that Herbert takes up in the compressed and subtle sonnet 'Christmas', beginning 'All after pleasures as I rid one day'.

Two basic ingredients of the genre are solitariness and fortuitousness of meeting, and these are extended in the ample meditation of poems like Wordsworth's 'Resolution and Independence' or Wilfred Owen's 'Strange Meeting'. In the process much is added, so that the 'epiphanic meeting' comes to have the status of a distinct subgenre. Its generic status is demonstrated by the fact that Roy Fuller can play with our expectation as, in 'Strange Meeting', an encounter in Boots the Chemists turns out to be with his own reflection in a mirror. (It is a poem which shows also how lyric topoi may be revivified by new combination; the contemplation of one's reflection in the mirror is itself a subgeneric convention in modern poetry.)

To extend the list of lyric subgenres would quickly swallow up the rest of this book (meditation on birds from Keats through Clare, Hardy and Wallace Stevens to Ted Hughes; hospital poems in the twentieth century; graveyard meditations – the list is infinite). Suffice it to say that the existence and gradual transformation of such subgenres is crucial to our reading experience.

Further distinctions between lyric genres can be made by criteria of diction and rhetoric. The hierarchic distinction between Pindaric and lesser lyric was made in part upon such grounds. Even in our own time it is still possible for poets to use deliberate clashes of stylistic register with specific lyric subjects. It is a characteristic feature (some might say indulgence) of Auden's poetic habit to use colloquial diction in formal contexts. It is, of course, a feature of the history of lyric, as of other poetic kinds, that successive generations have sought to revitalize poetic diction by conscious reaction to their predecessors. Elevation (as in the aureate diction of the fifteenth century, or the sublime of the eighteenth); inclusion (as in Donne's importation of sundry kinds of language into lyric, or the parallel efforts of modernist poets); cleansing (as in Ben Jonson's love of 'plain and neat language', or Wordsworth's aim to 'bring my language near to the language of men') – these are three characteristic strategies. For a reader the stylistic kind of a given poem is of considerable importance in directing his 'placing' of it in the lyric terrain.

Another distinction, which has come to seem especially significant in recent years (particularly to Marxist poets and critics) is that between poetry of community and poetry of the single voice. W. R. Johnson, for example, in *The Idea of Lyric* (Berkeley and London, 1982), argues that the privileging of private meditation in lyric poetry from the Renaissance to the modernists has been an unfortunate aberration from the 'choral' mode. Antony Easthope, in *Poetry as Discourse* (London, 1983), celebrates the death of 'bourgeois poetic discourse', 'the poetry of the "single voice"', and its replacement by poetry 'linked intimately with music and dancing, and so with a range of social institutions' (p. 161). Whatever one might think of the ideology (and myth-making nostalgia) which informs studies such as these, they do direct attention to a distinction which rightly takes the critic out of preoccupation only with words on a page to a consideration of the relationships of poet and audience, of the conditions within which lyric poetry is produced and the uses any society may make of it.

This division is related to, but by no means the same as, the separation of lyrics according to the nature of their presentation of the figure of the poet. The subjectivity or objectivity of lyric poems has, of course, figured as a central element in poets' own efforts to characterize their work (especially perhaps in the present century), and has been used as a central definition of lyric genres. Its critical significance means that Chapter 3 will be devoted to the subject.

Is there, then, any hope of defining 'lyric' as a generic label? The answer must be tentative. It must be accepted that a wide variety of determinants may properly be felt as significant in allocating a poem to a lyric category. While a 'personal' poem in stanza form about the pains of love and intended to be set to music would universally be accepted as a 'lyric', it is in no sense an authoritative model. For throughout literary history there has been not only a wide range of possible subject-matter, but considerable divergence in the criteria which have been felt as paramount (metrical, topical, presentational or functional), so that all decisions about a work's generic status must be conditioned by an awareness of that history. It is also inevitable that many poems might hover on the edges, and to pretend to a certainty that can judge infallibly between a lyrical narrative or a narrative lyric, an epigrammatic lyric or a lyrical epigram, would be to misunderstand the way readers actually use (or are used by) their generic awareness and the way poets play with and upon generic expectations. Finally it has to be acknowledged that from the nineteenth century onwards the distinction between 'lyric' and 'non-lyric' is much less important than subgeneric classifications within a much more loosely interpreted lyric umbrella.

IV

If it is difficult to demarcate the lyric as a genre or cluster of sub-genres, then to make sense of the applications of the modal term 'lyrical' is, in the end, virtually impossible. The ever increasing range of lyric subject-matter and variety of manner, together with the persistence of anachronistic Romantic criteria of lyric as universal, provide a vast semantic field from any corner of which a particular critic might glean the significance he attributes to the term.

If it is the musical connection which is felt to be primary, then the critic will have in mind poems that foreground the patterning of rhythm and sound, and will tend to speak of 'lyric smoothness', or else 'lyric purity'. If 'personal expression of feeling' is the mainspring, then 'lyrical intensity' will be the favoured term. If brevity and concentration are the key, then 'lyrical' will tend to be opposed to 'narrative' or 'dramatic'. And so one could go on. The adjective always encodes a selection from the historical variety of lyric, and its shorthand needs to be read with considerable care.

When the term is applied to non-poetic art forms (and indeed in the majority of off-hand critical uses) it is a combination of mellifluousness and feeling that is usually implied. So, while it would be precise to call *Romeo and Juliet* III.v 'lyrical', because its expression of feeling uses well-defined lyric topoi of the *aubade*, the film *Elvira Madigan* is called 'lyrical' because its concentration on a love affair, frequent scenes in rural setting and use of slow motion give it a narrative thinness made up for by a suspension of time and concentration upon images which is felt in some vague sense to be poetic. Something similar is happening when Virginia Woolf's novels are called 'lyrical' – it means only that arts of language and delineation of feeling are given priority over the 'normal' novelistic expectation of action and socially determined characterization. (Though Ralph Freedman, in *The Lyrical Novel* (Princeton, 1963), does develop a more substantial argument for the category.)

It is no doubt vain to hope for a ban on the modal use of 'lyrical' outside very specific contexts, but it is hard to see what effort of discrimination could make it useful.

2
Lyric and music

The poet, said Sir Philip Sidney, 'cometh to you with words set in delightful proportion, either accompanied with, or prepared for, the well enchanting skill of music' (Geoffrey Shepherd (ed.), *An Apology for Poetry*, London, 1965, p. 113). Ronsard, in similar vein, asserted that 'Poetry without instruments or without the grace of one or more voices is in no way appealing' (Paul Laumonier (ed.), *Art Poétique François, Oeuvres Completes*, XIV, Paris, 1949, p. 9). The connection asserted by them both is one that has occupied a perennial and special position in the definition of lyric genres. At the same time their linking has brought in its train multiple confusion, due in no small measure to the way several different kinds of argument have been derived from it, whose collusion promotes confusion rather than clarity.

The first argument states that 'true lyric is poetry written to be sung'. It follows, therefore, that the separation of lyric from music in Rome or in the later part of the sixteenth century marks a significant parting of the ways, and a fundamental division between 'songs' and 'literary lyrics'. This is the argument that underlies Mark Booth's *The Experience of Songs* (and might find some support from the way current usage differentiates between words for music and words for reading by using a plural form 'the lyrics' for the former).

The second argument notes that words are difficult for an audience to take in when they are sung, and derives from it the principle that 'musical' lyrics are necessarily 'simple, sensuous and passionate'. (Bruce Pattison's *Music and Poetry in the English Renaissance* develops this line, and Booth builds upon it.)

The third argument is rather different. It runs: lyrics that are in irregular rhythms are difficult for a composer to set, therefore only poems in regular, smooth and scrupulously repeated metres are 'musical'. Musical rhythm is opposed to speech rhythm. (John Hollander uses this argument of Donne in *Vision and Resonance*.)

When poets through the ages have used the label 'song' for a poem it usually signals the operation of criteria derived from arguments such as these. But as a basis for considering the nature of the relationship between lyric and music they are misleading.

To take each in turn. The separation of poems specifically written for music from the 'literary' lyric cannot be made absolute. Poets writing for print and private reading may yet be aware of music, may derive specific inspiration from it. Conversely, many poets who had no ear for music and who positively disliked their poems being set, produced lyrics that musicians and audiences have found ideal as songs. A. E. Housman is the most obvious example.

Secondly, lyrics written to be sung have not necessarily been simple. Pindar is scarcely noteworthy for the pellucidity of his style; the troubadours valued the complexity of the *trobar clus*. More importantly, it is not true that a song, any more than a play, is totally confined to simplicity by the fact of its single performance. The poet and songwriter, like the playwright, can have a reasonable expectation that their work will become sufficiently well known to individual members of their audience to be meditated upon and to have its subtleties appreciated.

Thirdly, the argument for metrical smoothness as essentially musical cannot stand if one simply looks at lyrics actually written to fit an existing tune, or at those which have taken shape at the same time as the music which accompanies them. From John Danyel's 'Eyes looke no more' to the lyrics of current 'pop' song, they are often sprawling, unmetrical assemblages, whose rhythms can only be reduced to system by a reader who already knows the tune. Verbal mellifluousness and musical rhythm are different things.

If we are to make sense of the connection between lyric and music it is important to distinguish carefully the precise nature of the interdependence that is being proposed. Even for those words actually prepared for musical setting it is necessary to divide words written to fit pre-existing tunes (liturgical sequence, broadside ballad or literary exercise) from those where music and words grow simultaneously (Cole Porter, Noel Coward, much of the popular song constructed in the recording studio) and from lyrics written first as poems and then set (the great majority of song lyrics, including those by poets who were also composers, like Machaut or Campion).

The next distinction is between lyrics destined for setting and those which declare an affiliation with the forms and conventions of song. In the latter, poets are gesturing towards a *literary* kind (the sort of words that are set to music), rather than subjecting themselves to the precise disciplines that settability imposes.

The third and most elusive category is that of lyrics one is disposed to consider 'musical', perhaps with the added support of biographical evidence of a given poet's knowledge of or fondness for music. Once this point is reached, new problems arise, which need to be investigated more fully. For what is considered 'musical' is very much determined by cultural assumptions that have varied profoundly at different times, with significant consequence for the ways in which poets and readers have felt about the musical connection of lyric poetry.

In the Renaissance it was believed that the power of music derived from the way its harmony reflected the harmony of the divine, the music of the spheres. By its power Orpheus made rocks, stones and trees to move, and was able to raise and calm the passions of men. When poetry was allied to music it partook of this divine power. It was also believed that the perfect fusion of poetry and music had been achieved in the classical period, when quantitative metres were allied to music which accurately set out the poetic rhythm. In various countries attempts were made to revive this imagined classical past. Thomas Campion, for example, defended quantitative metres in his *Observations*, and in *A Book of Ayres* produced one lyric with a musical setting which imitated the metre exactly. Significantly this is a poem in praise of God, the origin of the mystical harmony of creation:

> Come, let us sound with melody the praises,
> Of the kings king, th'omnipotent creator,
> Author of number, that hath all the world in
> Harmonie framed.

(ll. 1–4)

But though poetry achieved its greatest power when united with music, it was also true that, because music worked directly upon the passions, it was felt to be a potentially dangerous art, needing the control and direction that words could give it.

The attitudes which informed this view of the relationship between the sister arts began to erode during the seventeenth century (see John Hollander's excellent study, *The Untuning of the Sky*). But a sense that it was the words which guaranteed the moral worth of music persisted well into the eighteenth century. In 1744 James Harris wrote: 'Yet must it be remembered in this union, that poetry ever have the precedence, its utility as well as dignity being far the more considerable' (in Le Huray and Day, *Music and Aesthetics*, p. 39). Writing twenty-five years later, Daniel Webb argued:

> Music cannot of itself specify any particular passion. . . . But let eloquence cooperate with music and specify the motive of each particular impression . . . song takes possession of the soul, and general impressions become specific indications of the manners and the passions.

(in Le Huray and Day, op. cit., p. 119)

But Aikin, a little later, complained:

> The present age is characterised by a languid, sensual indolence, averse even in its pleasures to any thing that requires attention of

the mind. The ear, instead of being an avenue to the heart, expects to be gratified merely as an organ of sense, and the heroine, poetry, must give place to the harlot, music.

(*Essays on Song Writing*, 1810 edn, pp. 9–10)

His comments testify to the shift in relative status accorded to the two arts. As Abrams notes: 'in the theory of German writers of the 1790's, music came to be the art most immediately expressive of spirit and emotion, constituting the very pulse and quiddity of passion made public. . . . Hence the utility of music to define and illustrate the nature of poetry, particularly of the lyric' (*The Mirror and the Lamp*, p. 50). Music's triumph over words in the spontaneous expression of feeling is symbolized in the song of Wordsworth's 'Solitary Reaper'. The poet cannot hear her words, but if someone were to answer his question 'Will no one tell me what she sings?' it would be immaterial to the experience he describes. It is elemental feeling finding expression in musical sound that matters (as it does for Vaughan Williams in the wordless *vocalize* which begins his *Pastoral Symphony*).

In the aesthetics of the later nineteenth century music retained its primary place. Pater wrote:

Art, then, is thus always striving to be independent of the mere intelligence, to become a matter of pure perception, to get rid of its responsibilities to its subject or material; the ideal examples of poetry and painting being those in which the constituent elements of the composition are so welded together, that the material or subject no longer strikes the intellect only; nor the form, the eye or the ear only; but form and matter, in their union or identity, present one single effect to the 'imaginative reason', that complex faculty for which every thought and feeling is twin-born with its sensible analogue or symbol.

It is the art of music which most completely realises this artistic ideal, this perfect identification of form and matter. In its ideal, consummate moments, the end is not distinct from the expression; they inhere in and completely saturate each other,

and to it, therefore, to the condition of its perfect moments, all
the arts may be supposed constantly to tend and aspire.
(Donald L. Hill (ed.), *The Renaissance*, Berkeley,
Los Angeles and London, 1980, p. 109)

This statement completely inverts the assumptions of eighteenth-century and earlier aesthetics about the relative importance
of the sister arts. The attitudes it embodies persist through
symbolist poetry to Eliot or Wallace Stevens. (Though, of course,
there is transformation also, as a comparison of Wordsworth's
'Solitary Reaper' with the singer in Stevens's 'The Idea of Order at
Key West' makes clear. The focus shifts from song as pure feeling
to song as image of art's ordering power.)

This basic shift of attitude is of enormous consequence for the
lyric. From being poetry that organizes language so that it may
be accommodated to musical setting, lyric becomes language so
disposed that it imitates music in effect. Lyrics are poems that
work in some more or less precisely perceived way 'like' music,
with a consequent tendency to exclude from the category poems
that are narrative or didactic, whether or not they were actually
written to be set. Such attitudes did much to assist the elevation
of lyric in the generic hierarchy in the nineteenth century, and
contributed towards the promotion of feeling as a defining
characteristic of the lyric. We need, however, to be wary of the
strong pressure which assumptions derived from Romantic and
post-Romantic attitudes to the lyric/music relationship exert even
now upon us.

With all these cautions duly noted, we may turn to more detailed
consideration of some of the ways in which the relationships
between music and poetry have influenced and conditioned the
nature of lyric poems.

It is most obviously in the elements of formal organization that
connections are made between lyric and music, whether as a practical problem for the poet preparing words for setting, or as a
perceptual analogy upon which a lyric poet draws. Particularly is

this the case with features of repetition, and it is with some of them that this chapter will now be concerned.

One of the most frequent signals a poet may use to indicate a connection with musical forms is the adoption of a pattern of verse and chorus, or refrain. To a group of singing people the arrival of 'the chorus' generates a sense of release into the known and shared, and symbolizes community. This is true of the leader–chorus pattern of work songs, or of the sung responses in a liturgical litany, as it is of the invitation a music-hall singer offers to his audience to join in with a well-known chorus. In many musical forms – music-hall songs, theatrical 'musicals' and 'pop' songs – the distinction between verse and chorus is heavily marked by the subordination of a quasi-recitative verse to the 'big tune' of the chorus which we as audience are invited to know. Refrains and choruses can, of course, be nonsense syllables (from the 'fa la la' of the *ballet* to the 'Boom-bang-a-bang' of Eurovision Song Contest entries), but the relationship of varying verse to constant refrain can be deployed in many ways by poets.

Most obviously, perhaps, repetition can act as reinforcement of a message or insistent emphasis upon a poet's state of mind. Such is the case, for example, in lyrics like Dunbar's 'Lament for the Makaris' with its doleful 'timor mortis conturbat me'; Villon's celebrated and much imitated 'Ballade des dames du temps jadis', which gathers its pervasive *ubi sunt* in 'Mais où sont les neiges d'antan'; or Nashe's haunting 'Adieu, farewell earth's bliss' which links refrain with liturgical petition: 'I am sick, I must die: / Lord, have mercy upon us.' In these poems on mortality, and in many others that employ refrain, the effect is by repetition to generalize and universalize sentiment.

There are countless other possible uses for refrain. It may be linked to the verses as an answer to a series of questions, as in Bob Dylan's 'The answer, my friend, is blowin' in the wind', or may turn statements into question, as in Wyatt's 'What meaneth this?' The relationship may be contrastive, ironic, or simply enigmatic, as in some of Yeats's *Words for Music Perhaps*. The refrain may be spoken in the voice of the poet, or may enshrine some general truth against which a personal voice breaks, or may suggest a dialogue between different voices. However a poet may seek to develop and complicate the relationship of meaning between verse and refrain, it will always preserve the contrast between flux and stasis, escape and return, particular and general that is inbuilt in the original musical contrast between solo and chorus.

In the actual experience of listening to a song another kind of repetition is especially prominent – the echoing sound of rhyme. The frequent coincidence of rhyme words with the conclusion of musical phrases ensures their audibility in performance, and the fact that sound registers more immediately than sense means that even in very rapid singing the listener is aware of the existence of rhyme though meaning escapes him. Such is the case, for example, with W. S. Gilbert's 'patter' songs, where an audience is exhilarated by the sense of difficulty overcome, signalled by the triumph of rhyme.

In a musical context a basic paradox inherent in rhyme emerges very clearly. It is a mark of formal control, demonstrating the skill of the poet, ensuring that listeners are aware of his dexterity even in the face of music's tendency to absorb sense and dictate feeling. But at the same time, rhyme is a force for anarchy and misrule. The impulse Frye calls 'babble' finds outlet in the sportiveness of rhyme, the licence it gives for the exploitation of language's arbitrariness.

Rhymes end lines. In some medieval song-forms (ballade and rondeau for example) musical repetitions of phrase are matched by the patterns of rhyme. Of more general significance, however, is the way the variable lengths of musical units are echoed in words whose formal shape is defined by rhyme. If a poet provides words to fit music of any complexity then he will need to find some such structure. Sidney's poem 'To the tune of a Neapolitan song' is a typical example:

> No, no, no, no, I cannot hate my foe.
>   Although with cruell fire,

First throwne on my desire,
She sackes my rendred sprite.
   For so faire a flame embraces
     All the places
Where that heat of all heates springeth
     That it bringeth
To my dying heart some pleasure,
     Since his treasure
Burneth bright in fairest light. No, no, no, no.

                    (ll. 1–11)

This kind of variation of line-length was a generic signal for poems calling themselves 'madrigal' or 'ode'. Jonson's exquisite 'Slow, slow, fresh fount', written to be set to music, is an example of the first, and his 'Ode. To Sir William Sidney, on His Birthday', which is purely literary, an example of the second.

Two more recent examples illustrate the possibilities of rhyme for the lyricist, both of them celebrating the arbitrariness of rhyme in a way foreign to Sidney or Jonson. The first is the refrain from Cole Porter's 'You're the top':

You're the top!
You're the Colosseum,
You're the top!
You're the Louvr' Museum;
You're a melody
From a symphony
by Strauss;
You're a Bendel bonnet,
A Shakespeare sonnet,
You're Mickey Mouse.
You're the Nile,
You're the Tow'r of Pisa;
You're the smile
on the Mona Lisa.
I'm a worthless check,

> a total wreck,
> a flop,
> But if, Baby, I'm the bottom, You're the top!

Three features of the deployment of rhyme in this lyric deserve notice. First, the rhyme pattern aab, ccb of lines 5 to 10 is frequently found in words destined for musical setting. The subsidiary (or 'internal') rhymes correspond to the smaller units of the musical phrase. It is a favourite rhyme scheme for Thomas Campion, for example, and is employed by W. H. Auden in his 'Anthem for St. Cecilia's Day' written for Benjamin Britten:

> In a garden shady this holy lady
> With reverent cadence and subtle psalm,
> Like a black swan as death came on
> Poured forth her song in perfect calm.

> (ll. 1–4)

Second, rhyme is, to the listener especially, an anticipated goal. For a singer in extemporized (or quasi-extemporized) forms like the blues or calypso it is the fixed point at which he must somehow arrive. There is, therefore, a sense of tension released when the rhyme word is successfully reached. In music a delayed cadence has the same effect. When words and music are joined, the pleasurable suspense of longer phrases and correspondingly firmer closure when the delayed cadence is supported by the click of a rhyme word falling into place is a characteristic phenomenon. The last line of 'You're the top' is typical. In literary lyric rhyme alone may work the same effect. Donne's 'Sun Rising' opens:

> Busy old fool, unruly sun,
> Why dost thou thus
> Through windows, and through curtains call on us?

> (ll. 1–3)

Imagine how different it would feel if the third line began at 'through curtains'. Equally effective is the premature arrival of a rhyme. The Sapphic stanza, itself intended for musical setting, when anglicized with rhyme is tellingly used by many poets. Herbert's 'Vertue' is one variant:

> Sweet day, so cool, so calm, so bright,
> The bridal of the earth and sky,
> The dew shall weep thy fall tonight,
> For thou must die.

> (ll. 1–4)

The special prominence of rhyme in the aural experience of song means that it is possible to use the pursuit of a rhyme word as a device for promoting comic or bathetic effect. Many a translated opera libretto shows how easy it is to achieve unintentionally, but in Cole Porter's song the subtext of the refrain is 'You're anything I can think of that rhymes with what I've just said', and the high point of absurdity is reached when Mickey Mouse rhymes with Strauss. In literary lyric, then, the exploitation of the licence of rhyme can readily be used for comic or satiric purposes. John Fuller in 'Valentine' writes a comic blason poem which, incidentally, recalls the procedure of 'You're the top'. The eighth stanza is typical:

> I'd like to see you ironing your skirt
>   And cancelling other dates.
> I'd like to button up your shirt.
> I like the way your chest inflates.
> I'd like to soothe you when you're hurt
> Or frightened senseless by invert-
>   ebrates.

> (ll. 56–62)

Throughout the poem the arbitrariness of the order rhyme imposes on the listing of admired qualities suggests both naiveté (the writer dominated by his form) and yet at the same time the wit and control of John Fuller. In this stanza the extremity of the device of rhyming two halves of one word celebrates precisely this double possibility. In the *Façade* lyrics of Edith Sitwell, read artificially rhythmically over Walton's music, the arbitrary possibility of rhyme is used with gay abandon.

In the Cole Porter lyric rhyme units and sense units correspond. Noel Coward's 'Mad Dogs and Englishmen' is rather more varied:

> In tropical climes, there are certain times of day
> When all the citizens retire,
> To tear their clothes off and perspire.
> It's one of those rules that the greatest fools obey,
> Because the sun is much too sultry
> And one must avoid its ultry-vi'let ray.
>
> (ll. 1–6)

The patterning of this verse is intricate. Lines one and four are set to identical music. Their terminal rhyme therefore signals a functional similarity. Between them is a couplet, each line of which is set to rising scales in crotchet movement. The sixth line has closural force because of its rhyme with first and fourth, which have each been initiatory in both sense and musical implication. But the solidity of the closure is reinforced by the fact that just as lines one and four taken together manifest the familiar aab, ccb pattern, so the last line enfolds the couplet 'sultry / ultry', which at first promised to echo the independence of the couplet unit in lines two and three, within a ddb pattern. The formal similarity of the pattern of the last two lines to the pattern of first and fourth is reinforced by the fact that Coward, in a very characteristic manner, pushes sense on through the subsidiary rhyme words.

This example, whatever one might choose to think of its 'literary' merit, illustrates very well two basic qualities of rhyme. First, its capacity to delineate form. It is a small verification of Valéry's observation that 'Rhyme establishes a law independent of the poem's theme and might be compared to a clock outside it' (*The Art of Poetry*, Denise Folliot (trans.), New York, 1958, p. 125). But it also shows how the formal signal of rhyme can be played against the patterning of sense.

Both music and poetry depend upon the interplay of a number of different structuring elements. In music they are rhythm, melody, harmony and tonal structure. In poetry, rhyme, rhythm, grammatical and rhetorical structures. The tendency is for rhyme, because of its aural prominence in a listener's experience of song, to agree with the phrasal structure of the music (though the lightness of Coward's musical texture and his own characteristic mode of performance allow him to exploit the witty non-correspondence of subsidiary rhyme words with musical patterns). The difference between stanzas by Jonson, Herbert or Hardy, whether written to existing tunes, to be set, or as poems to be read, and the limp patterns of many 'pop' lyrics exposed in the pages of *Smash Hits* lies in their ability to manipulate rhyme in complex relationships with other systems of language to create self-sufficient and satisfying verbal structures. None the less it is true to say that lyric poetry characteristically foregrounds the quasi-musical patterning possibility of rhyme.

The other quality of lyric language that seems most to be influenced by music is, of course, rhythm. But, as the sprawliness of many *contrafacta* indicates, though music and poetry share in linearly established rhythmic patterns (unlike painting, to which the term 'rhythm' can only be applied metaphorically), musical and poetical rhythm are in many important respects quite different from one another. The temptingness of their similarity and the unfortunate fact of their difference have occasioned many a bitter and fruitless critical debate. It is vital to recognize at the outset that rhythm is a basic physiological fact, in the beat of the heart, and a physical possibility in marching or dance. It has a fundamental psychological effect as stimulant or tranquillizer. It is misleading to speak as if poetry derived its rhythmicality from music, for both are issues of the same underlying impulse realized in different media.

In classical literature musical accompaniment probably had a determining force in making the quantitative metres of verse accessible to the ear of the listener. Such was certainly the case in

Renaissance quantitative experiments, where Campion or Baïf expected their music to clarify a metrical structure which they did not expect a reader to be able to recognize aurally. A modern example of a poetic rhythm defined by the music which accompanies it is Linton Kwesi Johnson's 'Reggae Sounds':

> Shock-black bubble-doun-beat bouncing
> rock-wise tumble-doun sound music
> foot-drop find drum, blood story
> bass history is a moving
> is a hurting black story.

(ll. 1–5)

Beyond examples such as these (with perhaps the addition of ballads by Burns or Hardy, written with specific tunes in mind) the nature of the connection between musical and poetical rhythm is a subject of great complexity. (Not least of the problems is the fact that different languages work rhythmically in different ways. Everything that follows is, if true, true of English, and makes no claim to apply to other languages.)

The chief difference between musical and poetic rhythm lies in the fact that a musician may fill the space between pulses that (since the mid-seventeenth century at least) mark out regular bar-units with any number of notes in different rhythmic groupings, where the poet is confined by the impossibility of persuading the English ear not to supply secondary accent after a maximum of two unstressed syllables, and by the imprecision of the graphic presentation of words in indicating the poet's preferred rhythmic realization of a line whose monosyllables make for ambiguity. (It is revealing that composers from Campion to Castelnuovo-Tedesco complain of the clogging effect of monosyllables, and characteristic that Hopkins, for whom musical analogy was an important stimulus to rhythmic experiment, resorted to diacritics in an attempt to deal with the problem.)

None the less, poetry which emphasizes a regular beat is often felt to be that which is most obviously connected with music.

The jog-trot metres of hymnody are a case in point. Lowell's observations in 'Waking Early Sunday Morning' are relevant here:

> O Bible chopped and crucified
> in hymns we hear but do not read,
> none of the milder subtleties
> of grace or art will sweeten these
> stiff quatrains shovelled out four-square –
> they sing of peace, and preach despair;
> yet they gave darkness some control,
> and left a loophole for the soul.
>
> (ll. 49–56)

This stanza, whatever its place in Lowell's larger meditation, characterizes accurately the paradox of all metrically ordered language – that it enforces control, but at the same time permits a liberation for the 'soul'. This is the heart of its affinity with musical rhythm.

It is especially true that poems in triple rhythms carry a suggestion of music (not least because 3/4 time is easy in music, but difficult to sustain in English, with its preference for alternation of stress and unstress). Examples can be found in all kinds of lyric, from Gilbert's:

> When you're lying awake with a dismal headache,
> and repose is taboo'd by anxiety;
> I conceive you may use any language you choose
> to indulge in without impropriety.
>
> ('The Nightmare Song', *Iolanthe*, ll. 1–4)

or Smith's hymn:

> Immortal, invisible, God only wise;
> In light inaccessible, hid from our eyes.
>
> (ll. 1–2)

to Swinburne's *Hymn to Proserpine*:

> Thou hast conquered, O pale Galilean; the world has grown
>   gray from thy breath;
> We have drunken of things Lethean, and fed on the fullness
>   of death.

(ll. 35–6)

Triple rhythms frequently figure in the work of poets writing literary versions of ballad, from Blake's *Songs*, through Browning's 'How they brought the Good News' to Kipling's 'The Ladies', with its memorable conclusion: 'For the Colonel's Lady an' Judy O'Grady / Are sisters under their skins.'

In general the tendency is to call any metrical structure that is regular and smooth 'musical', and to oppose it to the irregularities of 'speech rhythm'. 'Musical' lyric is artificial, where the pressure of deep feeling requires passionate directness. But such codification is false to the nature of poetic rhythm and seriously misleading in its suggestion of the way a reader might feel a 'musical' relationship. Northrop Frye takes issue with these assumptions in the *Anatomy of Criticism*. He argues that if rhythm organized by regular pulse is what characterizes music, then that poetry is most musical which fills the space between pulses with irregular numbers of syllables. Pulse then plays against the regular pattern of accentual/syllabic metre. His argument is refreshing, and properly rescues the versification of Wyatt, Donne and Browning from inappropriate censure. But its straightforward reversal of usual prejudice does not in the end prove satisfactory.

Clarification of the issues can only come when certain wrong assumptions are dispelled. First, the opposition between 'musical' and 'speech' rhythms is illusory. All poetic rhythm is determined by the rhythms of English speech, whether more or less systematized. Second, the rhythms of music and of poetry are essentially different. Where music is flexible, language is constrained; where language is infinitely various, music is bound to specified note-lengths. It is this which accounts for the failure of all attempts to scan poetry by musical notation, but also accounts for Roy Fuller's envy of the flexibility of musical rhythm in his essay 'Fascinating Rhythm' from *Owls and Artificers*. It is precisely because they are different that the test of setting words is challenging to the composer, and the stimulus of music fruitful for the poet. It follows therefore that, though the rhythmical germ of a poem may be musical (as many poets have asserted), the resultant lyric always represents an accommodation of one kind of rhythm to another.

The true affinity of poetic rhythm with that of music, therefore, lies not in metre or rhythm abstracted from words, but in the subtlety with which a poet deploys the resources of a language's rhythmic possibility in relationship with meaning, syntax, rhyme and other patterns of sound. A satisfying musical tune may be rhythmically simple, but achieve its effect through a subtle deployment of music's other resources (as is the case in folk-song, the lute airs of Campion or many Schubert songs, for example). A simple metrical base becomes musical only when it similarly reacts with other systems of organization. Conversely, a poem fails to be 'musical' either when regular rhythm mindlessly coerces meaning or syntax, or when no rhythmic organization is perceptible, just as a piece of music fails when melody is predictable, rhythm relentless and harmony conventional.

All of this means that we have to recognize the fundamentally metaphoric status of any assertion about a poem's 'musicality', and consequently to accept that a poem we would wish to call musical may have been written by a poet who learnt to use his rhythms from his experience of reading other poems rather than from listening to music. It must, in the end, be a term for a critic to deploy, not a statement about a poem's actual genesis.

It is significant that apologists for free (or free-er) verse have found musical analogy useful in describing the nature of their enterprise. F. S. Flint's rules for imagist poets suggest it is right 'as regarding rhythm: to compose in sequence of the musical phrase, not in sequence of a metronome', a prescription Pound extended: 'behave as a musician, when dealing with that phase of your art which has exact parallels in music' (Peter Jones (ed.), *Imagist Poetry*, Harmondsworth, 1972, pp. 129, 133 respectively). William Carlos Williams speaks of the 'tune which the lines make in our ears', and asserts 'by its *music* shall the best of modern verse be known and the *resources* of the music' (James Scully, *Modern Poets on Modern Poetry*, London, 1966, p. 71). Donald Davie indeed goes as far as to distinguish free-verse composition as 'musical', from metrical composition as 'architectural' (*Agenda*, Rhythm Double Issue, 10/11, 1972–3, pp. 17–18).

A poetic structure whose unit is the line rather than the regularly recurrent 'foot', whose typographic representation upon the page therefore becomes, in Olson's words, a 'score' for the reader (Scully, op. cit., p. 278), places great weight upon line-endings as signals of intonation patterns and throws upon the reader the responsibility for finding rhythms that justify the claims for attention that the poem's shape makes. It is still important that rhythm is felt as fruitfully reacting with other systems of formal organization. A very simple example is given by lines from Williams's 'To a Poor Old Woman':

> munching a plum on
> the street a paper bag
> of them in her hand
>
> They taste good to her
> They taste good
> to her. They taste
> good to her

(ll. 1–7)

The variously arranged repetition of the second 'stanza' draws attention to the way rhythmic decision determines tone and implication, while the fact of repetition itself suits the way the woman receives 'a solace of ripe plums'.

The characteristic vices of free and metrical verse are complementary. The order of metre may become monotonous and its failure will tend to provoke scorn at the poet incompetently dis-torting language upon a rack of rhythm. The liberty of free verse may become rhythmically vacuous, and its failure provoke annoy-ance that we should be compelled to search for a system that is not there. The successes of both will derive from the revelatory possi-bilities of the play of language's systems. As Susanne Langer observes, in *Feeling and Form* (London, 1953): 'the fullest exploi-tation of language sound and rhythm, assonance and sensuous associations, is made in lyric poetry' (p. 258). Though all poetry uses such resources, it is a defining feature of most lyric genres that they are firmly foregrounded in a way that would be unhelpful in other poetic kinds.

Thus far we have considered the formal elements of lyric that might be said to have a musical analogy. As least as important is the effect that writing words for musical setting has upon the dis-position of meaning. The lyric intended to be sung character-istically respects the difficulty a singer faces if he is called upon to carry sense across a musical cadence, and tends therefore to be chary of enjambement. A listener tends to be aware of discrete units of sense contained within individual musical phrases, and not to worry too much about the continuity of meaning from phrase to phrase. Consequently end-stopped lines and paratactic relationships are the norm of the libretto lyric. Barbara H. Smith notes this characteristic of song verse in *Poetic Closure*, and dis-cusses the way it tends to lead to larger structures based on simple patterns like 'the list' or 'variations on a theme'. Poets writing literary 'songs' will tend to seize on these structural models as generic markers.

The discrete units of words-for-music do, however, offer positive opportunities to the lyric poet. Though in many a song the gaps between verbal phrases are merely a shelter for *non sequitur* or an opportunity to heap up slabs of prefabricated emotional catch-phrases, a poet may choose to exploit the lack of connectedness, to tease the reader's assumption that at some level a lyric poem must 'make sense', and thereby illuminate the significance of detail or image. It is this which gives numinous quality to the detail of many a ballad, which invests Wyatt's 'They flee from me' with its power. It is also a possibility infinitely exploited by symbolists, imagists and their contemporary descendants. The grounds for their adventure are various, but among them is a claim that fragmentation, rupture of syntax and concentration upon image enables poetry to take to itself something of the way of music's working.

Disjunctiveness of line or sense units is one exploitable possibility. So too are relationships between stanza units. A lyric for music, if successive stanzas are to be sung to the same tune, must fit equally well throughout. The demands this makes have been discussed by writers such as Catherine Ing in *Elizabethan Lyrics* and Bruce Pattison in *Music and Poetry of the English Renaissance*, who demonstrate how many Elizabethan lyricists duly and craftily satisfied the prescription.

A poet not writing for music can choose to exploit stanzaic form in two further ways. Because each stanza is a new start, the lacunae between stanzas may be seized upon and turned to advantage. The argument of many of Donne's lyrics, for example, depends upon unstated shifts of stance between stanzas, or upon the imagined interjection of an absent interrogator. The evolution of a lyric's implied narrative or pattern of feeling frequently becomes available to a reader only when he makes a creative effort to supply the gaps created by the leap from stanza to stanza. On the other hand, the repetition of stanza form may be accepted as a way of reinforcing feeling, intensifying the presentation of a state of mind.

Music, then, is not in any direct way a 'source' for lyric. Myths of perfect fusion in Ancient Greece or pre-Renaissance oral literature are delusive. But the techniques of accommodation developed in poems composed with or written to be set to music remain as possibilities that the writer of 'literary' lyric may imitate. Furthermore any individual poet may find music stimulating, though it issues indirectly in a poem upon a page. Finally a critic may usefully use the way music's organizational systems work in fruitful relationship as an analogy to characterize the successful play of structuring elements in lyric poems.

Slightly fuller consideration of two poems from different centuries, neither written to be set to music, but both composed by poets whose love of music is well attested, may serve to draw together some of the threads of this chapter.

The first is George Herbert's 'Easter':

> Rise heart; thy Lord is risen. Sing his praise
> > Without delays,
> Who takes thee by the hand, that thou likewise
> > With him mayst rise:
> That, as his death calcined thee to dust,
> His life may make thee gold, and much more just.
>
> Awake, my lute, and struggle for thy part
> > With all thy art.
> The crosse taught all wood to resound his name,
> > Who bore the same.
> His stretched sinews taught all strings, what key
> Is best to celebrate this most high day.
>
> Consort both heart and lute, and twist a song
> > Pleasant and long:
> Or since all music is but three parts vied
> > And multiplied;
> O let thy blessed Spirit bear a part
> And make up our defects with his sweet art.

This poem is a prelude to the obviously 'song-like' lyric 'I got me flowers to straw thy way'. It acts as both invocation and imitation of music as a response to Easter. As in many Herbert lyrics, form is iconic. The three stanzas image the three parts of music. Their separate, parallel identity is ensured by the formal device of beginning each with an imperative verb, while the sequence 'heart', 'lute', 'heart plus lute plus Holy Spirit' ties them into satisfying additive structure.

The musicality of the poem does not reside in any obvious rhythmic irregularity. It is in the phrasing, in the relationship of patterns of meaning to the verse form, and in the deflection of too relentless a beat by the varied deployment of monosyllables that Herbert's musical art is demonstrated.

There is, for example, a purposeful modulation of the imperative opening to each stanza. The first, 'Rise heart', is rhythmically ambiguous as the two monosyllables compete for the stronger stress, and the brevity of the injunction gives force to its appeal. In the second stanza 'Awake my lute' is gentler in its straightforward iambic rhythm, while 'Consort both heart and lute', with its longer sense-unit, relaxes imperative force as the poem moves towards its conclusion.

The variation of the final couplets of each stanza works in a similarly controlled fashion. In the first stanza the two lines are held together by an image proposed in the first and explained in the second. There is no enjambement; the last line is broken into two units. The second stanza compresses simile into metaphor, and by enjambement pushes the reader into a continuous last line. The final stanza is quieter, its image less enforced, and serene closure is engendered by the settling of sense into two elements each securely filling the pentameter frame with a continuous sense-unit.

Throughout the poem Herbert shows his dexterity in the flexible handling of long and short lines. The ebb and flow of sense across rhyme-signalled line endings gives the lyric its necessary variation. The strength of enjambement is varied; syntactical relationships are of different kinds. All this makes the poem 'musical', as well as having music as its emblematic topic. Herbert here celebrates the satisfaction of form as reifying his meaning. In other poems, 'The Deniall' or 'Grief' for example, he wrestles with the problem that verses may seem 'too fine a thing for my rough sorrows', but whether positively or negatively, Herbert's iconic purposes never inhibit his musically dynamic versification.

The second example comes from Geoffrey Hill's sequence *The Pentecost Castle*. The poems were prompted by both musical and literary stimuli. The structure of the sequence as a whole is described by the poet in these terms:

> It's a hinted drama. One or two critics have suggested that a coherent, consecutive drama is being conveyed: I don't think it's so. I had no such intention; there's no plot but there are little shadowy hints of one.
>
> (John Haffenden (ed.), *Viewpoints*, London, 1981, pp. 91–2)

The shadowiness that informs the collection can also be seen in the twelfth lyric from the sequence:

> Married and not for love
> you of all women
> you of all women
> my soul's darling my love
>
> faithful to my desire
> lost in the dream's grasp where
> shall I find you everywhere
> unmatched in my desire
>
> each of us dispossessed
> so richly in my sleep
> I rise out of my sleep
> crying like one possessed

Formally this poem is solidly made. Nearly all the 'rhymes' are full verbal repetition. As in the Herbert lyric the new start and parallel status of each stanza is emphasized by similarity, here of rhythm. The poem ends securely as, for the first time, the initiatory rhythm common to each stanza recurs at the end. Within this firm shape rhythmic fluctuation is subtly handled in the patterning of two- and three-syllable units.

Throughout the lyric, however, this formal solidity plays against elusiveness of meaning. The poem deploys, as Hill says, the 'conventional phraseology and idiom' of the Spanish folk songs

he was adapting. It gestures towards familiar topoi of love poetry –
love of a married woman; the dreamt image; the awakening – but
the reader cannot securely construct a situation to which the poem
as a whole might be construed as a response. Instead the lyrical
tendency to isolate line-units is compounded by syntactic indeterminacy. In the first stanza the repeated 'you of all women' chal-
lenges the reader to choose from amongst its possible inflections as
he wonders about the connection of lines one and two, three and
four. This is a phenomenon precisely analogous to the way in
music that recapitulation of a phrase becomes a new initiation.
The tension is particularly marked in the central lines of the
second stanza, where uncertainty about how to punctuate the
sense gives especial hovering force to enjambement. Even the
firmness of rhythmic closure at the end of the poem is undermined
by the pain of the sentiment and the pun of the final word.

This lyric is typical of the sequence as a whole, where the formal
devices of rhyme, half-rhyme, repetition and rhythmic pattern
play with and against syntax, image and sense. It is precisely the
formal control that permits us to entertain and respond to the
liberation of feeling and response that the shadowiness of the
'drama' necessitates.

Those two poems, for all their substantial difference, exemplify
what seems to me truly 'musical' lyric. Music can serve poets in
many ways. It can provide a formal model for poems large (like
Four Quartets) or small (Denise Levertov's 'Variations'). It can be
wittily gestured towards and represented in poems which have a
musical theme (Wallace Stevens's 'Peter Quince at the Clavier' or
some of the lyrics in John Fuller's *Waiting for the Music*). But, as
Auden rightly asserts, the critic must always recognize 'Man is an
analogy-drawing animal; that is his great good fortune. His danger
is of treating analogies as identities, of saying, for instance,
"Poetry should be as much like music as possible"' (*The Dyer's
Hand*, London, 1963, p. 52).

3
The lyric 'I'

The OED definition of lyric juxtaposes 'meant to be sung' with 'the name for short poems . . . directly expressing the poet's own thoughts and sentiments'. The last chapter explored some of the implications of the first quality; this seeks to subvert the second by a consideration of the variousness of the ways in which lyric poems deploy a first-person speaker.

A naif acceptance of the OED definition underlies much of what is taught to children in schools as creative writing, and prompts many a student searching for ways to write essays on poetry to retreat to biographies to help them fill out the 'I' of the lyric. But, as Barbara H. Smith insists, all poetry is 'fictive discourse', and therefore:

> The interpretation of a poem as a *historical* utterance may serve the special purposes of the literary historian or biographer, but is likely to appear shallow, reductive, or 'literal-minded' precisely to the degree that it restricts the context of the poem to historical particulars and suggests that the meanings of the poem are to be located exclusively in a historically determinate context.
>
> (*On the Margins of Discourse*, Chicago, 1978, pp. 34–5)

It has been one of the principal aims of literary criticism for the last half-century or so to displace the appeal to the author as a validation of our interpretation of literature. It is commonplace to see the lyric speaker as a 'persona' adopted by a poet. The next step is to accept that 'the poetic persona is a construct, a function of the language of the poem', though, as Culler goes on to say, this reader-constructed persona 'none the less fulfils the unifying role of the individual subject, and even poems which make it difficult to construct a poetic persona rely for their effects on the fact that the reader will try to construct an enunciative posture' (*Structuralist Poetics*, p. 170).

The persona can be presented in a variety of activities – doing, thinking, writing or speaking – and may or may not be explicitly present. From the evidence of the words on the page the reader deduces the 'virtual narrative' of the speaker's actions or thoughts.

Developing a notion of 'persona' does not, however, solve all problems. For at different periods of literary history the relationship between persona and poet has been represented, albeit fictively, as sometimes more, sometimes less independent. Shelley prefaced his 'Ode to the West Wind' with the statement that 'This poem was conceived and chiefly written in a wood that skirts the Arno, near Florence, and on a day when that tempestuous wind . . . was collecting the vapours which pour down the autumnal rains'. In very similar fashion Wordsworth entitled a poem 'Lines Composed a Few Miles Above Tintern Abbey On Revisiting the Banks of the Wye During a Tour. July 13, 1798'. These titles act to enforce the identification of persona with poet, and to affirm the 'historical' origin of a particular poem. That they do so accords with Wordsworth's famous definition of poetry as 'the spontaneous overflow of powerful feeling', or with Shelley's assertion that 'Poetry is the record of the best and happiest moments of the happiest and best minds.' Whether objectively true or not, the biographical information leads a reader to view the speaker of the poem, and the language he uses, in a specific way – that of 'a man speaking to men' – with the words on the page a transparent medium conveying the thoughts of the poet to the mind of the reader.

This is not the only kind of contract a poem may make with a reader. It belongs in a particular culture, and in considering the history of lyric poetry it is necessary to consider other possible relationships.

It is important to recognize also the ways in which the reader's construction of a persona is conditioned by factors other than the words on a page. We might feel that our understanding of the first-person speaker of a poem read in a book is rather different from that which we might have of the same poem delivered by the poet at a public reading. Even more must it have been the case that the relationship between poet, persona and poem was different when a troubadour performed in front of his courtly hosts. So too, the poem written for manuscript circulation amongst 'private friends' permits a relationship both more precise and yet more flexible than that encountered in the anonymity of print. A sung lyric invites a communal identification of singer and audience that is distinct from the experience of individual private reading.

Also significant is the kind of speech which a poem presents to us. The 'I' may speak directly to the reader; more often the lyric is addressed to a recipient different from the audience – to a lover, to an object, to an abstraction, so that, in Mill's definition, 'a lyric is not heard but overheard'; or the lyric 'I' might be construed as a voice 'talking to itself, or to nobody'.

All these, as well as criteria of use and function, play their part in informing the reader's understanding of the relationship of poet–persona–poem–audience.

*

The reader opening an anthology of troubadour lyrics will find there many poems that speak directly to a single female recipient, poems expressing a first-person response to love or the cycle of nature. Bernard de Ventadour's 'Chantars no pot gaire valer' opens with a profession of 'sincerity':

Singing cannot much avail, if from within the heart comes not the song; nor can the song come from the heart, unless there be there noble love, heartfelt. Hence is my singing supreme, for in love's joy I hold and direct my mouth, my eyes, my heart, my understanding.

(Alan R. Press, *Anthology of Troubadour Lyric Poetry*, Edinburgh, 1971, p. 67)

But the troubadours were, in the main, professional poets, performing their songs to music before a number of different audiences. They and their audiences were aware that the songs were transferable, to be sung by others and addressed to the lady of the house, whomsoever she might be. These lyrics are, therefore, unambiguously dramatic performances. At the same time, the thematic material of troubadour lyric was highly conventionalized. This means that a characteristic assertion of the poets is to identify themselves as craftsmen, and the audience then delights in the mastery of complex patterns of rhyme and repetition, and the manipulation of standard ideas.

This does not, of course, mean that troubadour poetry is necessarily frigid. Giraut de Borneil's 'Reis glorios' (in Press, op. cit., pp. 150–1), an *aubade* of telling simplicity and directness, with its haunting refrain 'Et ades sera l'alba' ('and soon it will be dawn') is but one contrary example. Peter Dronke draws attention, in his survey *The Medieval Lyric* (London, 1968), to many fine poems. But, as he says, their achievement is to attain 'a certain dramatic objectivity'.

John Burrow, surveying medieval lyric poems employing the first-person speaker, declares the OED definition with which this chapter began to be 'quite inapplicable to the lyric poetry of the Middle Ages' and proceeds to describe some of the possibilities that were deployed: the 'I' who is 'to be understood not as the poet himself, nor as any other individual speaker, but as a lover, a penitent sinner, or a devotee of the Virgin'; the fully dramatic 'I' which requires the reader 'not to identify with, but to *identify* the speaker' (*Medieval Writers and their Work*, Oxford, 1982, pp. 67–8).

'Friar Thomas de Hales' Love Ron' (Rune) illustrates a further possibility. The poet explains that he has been commissioned by a

maid of Christ's' to teach her how to take Christ as her lover, and
sserts 'ich hire wule teche as ic con'. It is, then, an explicitly
didactic poem in which the first-person speaker addresses the
maiden directly as he urges upon her the frailty of earthly love and
he desirability of Christ. Persona and poet are identical, and the
ending makes the function of the poem quite clear:

> This rym, mayde, ich thee sende
>   open and withoute seal;
> *ask*   Bidde ic that thou it untrende   *unroll*
> *learn without*   & leorny but book each del;   *part*
>   Hereof that thou be swithe hende   *courteous*
>   & teach it other maydencs wel.
> *nows*   Who-so cuthe it to than ende,
>   It wolde him stonde muchel stel.   *afford great help*
>
> When thou sittest in longynge
>   draw thou forth this ilke wryt;
> *with, voice*   Mid swete stephne thou it singe,
>   & do al so it thee byt.   *commands*
>
>   (Carleton Brown, *Religious Lyrics of the Fourteenth
>   Century*, Oxford, 1939, p. 74, spelling partly
>   modernized)

It is a poem to be used to stiffen the spiritual will of the maiden; it
is a poem to be shared; it is a poem to be learnt as a kind of
mnemonic (and also, it seems, as a kind of charm). The skill of the
poet is shown in the lyric's artful deployment of conventional
motifs: an extended *ubi sunt* ('Hwer is paris & heleyne / that weren
so bryht and feyre on bleo); treatment of Christ as lover and so on.
It is a product of a time when, as Douglas Gray puts it:

> The lyrics are sometimes put to what we might recognize as
> 'literary' uses (e.g. in plays), but more often than not the
> impulse behind them is quite functional and practical. Utility is
> normally put before beauty, and sometimes, though fortunately

not always, excludes it altogether. The lyrics were meant to be
and were, used, sometimes in private devotion and prayer
sometimes for public devotional display, sometimes to empha
size and drive home points in sermons.

> (*Themes and Images*, London, 1972, p. 37

It is in this context that the lyrics where Christ or the Virgin Mar
are the dramatic speakers must be placed. But the functional natur
of medieval lyric does not preclude the exercise of imagination
Indeed the exercise of the faculty of 'making images' was precisel
that which affective meditation encouraged. A lyric which uses the
basic (and conventional) idea of Christ as the lover of mankind i
given intensity of application by the brief presence of the poet:

> In the vaile of restles mynd
>> I sowght in mownteyn and in mede,
> Trustyng a treulofe for to fynd.
>> Upon an hyll than toke I hede,
>> A vois I herd (and nere I yede)   *went*
> In gret dolour complaynyng tho,
>> 'See, dere soule, my sydes blede,
> *Quia amore langueo.'*   *Because I languish*
>> *for love*
>>> (ll. 1–8, in Gray, *A Selection of Religious Lyrics*
>>> Oxford, 1975, p. 41

This variation of the *chanson d'aventure* opening locates the poem i
the mind of the poet (linking it with the dream-vision poems whic
characteristically explored the powers of fantasy and visionar
illumination). The fact that the poet presents himself as 'seeking
bestows a quasi-dialogic character on Christ's speech, particulariz
ing his address to 'mannys soule'. The fruitfulness of this 'placing' o
poet and Christ can be seen in two later stanzas of the poem:

> 'I sitt on an hille for to se farre
>> I loke to the vayle; my spouse I see:
> Now rynne she awayward, now cummyth she narre,

Yet from myn eye-sight she may nat be.
Sum waite ther pray, to make hyr flee –
I rynne tofore to chastise hyr foo.
Recover, my soule, agayne to me,
Quia amore langueo.

'My swete spouse, will we goo play?
Apples ben rype in my gardine;
I shall clothe the in new array,
Thy mete shall be mylk, honye and wyne.
Now, dere soule, latt us go dyne;
Thy sustenance is in my crippe – loo!   bag
Tary not now, fayre spouse myne,
Quia amore langueo

(ll. 73–88)

The meditative quality of this poem, the intimacy and warmth of feeling it enables are particularly appealing – though less subjective poems of praise in high style, of which Dunbar's 'Haile, sterne superne' is a fine example, have their rewards. But this devotional poem is individual in its skill and personal in its application in a manner quite distinct from the strikingly idiosyncratic *Holy Sonnets* of John Donne.

The same is true of an apparently more directly personal meditation like this:

Whan I thinke on Cristes blod
That he schad upon the rode,
    I lete teris smerte.
What man may be onkende   *unkind*
That Cristis blod hath in mende   *mind*
    And enterly in his herte.

(ll. 1–6, in Gray, op. cit., p. 34)

is a translation of a Latin hymn, and the 'I' of this lyric has the same universal status as that which a congregation of singing

Christians affords to the first-person pronoun of a hymn lik
Watts's 'When I survey the wondrous cross'.

One final example may extend (without in any way claiming t
exhaust) the possibilities that medieval lyric poets explored. /
poem on the theme of mortality begins:

> Farewell, this world! I take my leve for evere;
> I am arested to apere at Goddes face.
> O myghtfull God, thou knowest that I had levere   *rathe*
> Than all this world to have oone houre space
> To make asythe for all my grete trespace.   *reparatio*
>   (ll. 1–5, in Gray, op. cit., p. 9?

This is conventional enough, and the 'I' is of Burrow's first kinc
though the casting of the lyric gives it a certain dramatic urgency
The second stanza takes a slightly different direction:

> This lyfe, I see, is but a cheyre feyre;   *cherr*
>   All thyngis passene and so most I algate.   *in any ca*
> Today I sat full ryall in a cheyere,   *roy*
>   Tyll sotell deth knokyd at my gate,
>   And onavysed he seyd to me, 'Chek-mate'.   *without warnin*
> Lo, how sotell he maketh a devors!   *separatio*
> And wormys to fede, he hath here leyd my cors.
>   (ll. 8–1⁴

In line three the speaker seems to furnish circumstantial deta
about 'himself'. But the poem is simply adopting one of the cor
ventional voices of the Dance of Death, and, as the last line of th
stanza indicates, is moving into the specific category of 'warning
from the tomb'.

The movement is confirmed and movingly elaborated in the
next two stanzas, beginning:

> Speke softe, ye folk, for I am leyd aslepe!
> I have my dreme – in trust is moche treson.
>
> (ll. 15–16)

But the poem concludes with a return to the voice of a man near
death:

> Farewell, my frendis! the tide abideth no man:
> I moste departe hens, and so shall ye.
>
> (ll. 29–30)

It is homiletic in the way that a morality play like *Everyman* is
minatory.

There is, then, no single location of the 'I' of this poem. The
speaker is alive–dead–alive; particular and universal. The poem
does not read like the deliberately decentred poems of recent years
because the reader accommodates this variation both within literary conventions of the period, and within the didactic function of
the whole – to teach us how to die.

But however one may insist that the first-person speaker in
medieval lyric is generalized or dramatic, there remain poems
where identity of speaker and sentiment, and reference of both to a
historical moment, are unavoidable. From the farewell song of
William of Poitou to the *Testaments* of Villon, one can find
personae that resist too ready a dissolution. The reader is persuaded that conventions of lyric have offered an individual a way
of coping with experience.

Even more is this the case in Renaissance lyric. For while the
convention of lyric as an epideictic kind – praising sovereign or
lover – is of enormous significance, and though many lyrics were
written for performance with music in a social environment, an
increasing number of poems seem to offer the reader a coherently

projected individual speaking-voice. It is often seen as the distinguishing mark of the poetry of Wyatt that it injects a note of personal experience into the medieval conventions that it takes over and redeploys. Later in the sixteenth century it is Donne's weeding of the Petrarchan garden that is most often remarked as his individual and anti-conventional characteristic.

In part this sense of individuality is produced by statements that seem inexplicable except in terms of some particular circumstance in the poet's life. Shakespeare's enigmatic Sonnet 125, beginning 'Were it aught to me I bore the canopy' is one such case. We also find references to the writing of poetry as a private, meditative activity. Sidney's *Astrophil and Stella*, Sonnet 34 begins:

> Come, let me write. 'And to what end?' To ease
>   A burdened heart.

Sonnet 44 claims: 'My words I know do well set forth my mind'

But, of course, to try to read Renaissance lyric poetry as if the 'I' is synonymous with the poet is to invite the kind of disillusion that affected Sidney Lee at the beginning of this century when he discovered that many of the poems in the Elizabethan sonnet sequences were detailed imitations of continental models, thus, as he saw it, undermining the claims to 'sincerity' that their writers made.

It is not, however, sufficient to run away from the problem merely by asserting that all Renaissance poetry must be read as essentially dramatic, projecting a constructed 'persona' to the reader. For to do so runs the risk of detaching these lyrics from their historical circumstance, and thus of misrepresenting them as seriously as a naively neo-Romantic attitude can do.

John Stevens in *Music and Poetry in the Early Tudor Court* has amply demonstrated how the early lyric poetry of the Renaissance, sharing often both popular and more learned antecedents, makes best sense when seen in a reconstructed social context – the courtly 'game of love'. Many of the lute songs of the later part of the period also had their origins in domestic, social circumstances,

Campion records that many of his songs were composed in the household of Sir Thomas Monson; John Danyel dedicated his *Songs* of 1606 to Mrs Anne Grene in these words:

> That which was onely privately compos'd
> For your delight, Faire Ornament of Worth,
> Is here come to bee publickely disclos'd,
> And to an universall view put forth.
> Which having beene but yours and mine before,
> (Or but of few besides) is made hereby
> To bee the worlds: and yours and mine no more.

It is vital to our comprehension of the literary lyric of the period that a great deal of it, like these songs, had an audience originally small and known to the writer. For the age was one of transition from manuscript to print. Most of the lyric poets now enshrined in the canon did not design their poetry to be published before an anonymous public, but circulated poems in manuscript amongst their private friends.

There are three important consequences of this basic observation. In the first place, poets writing for a known audience are, perhaps paradoxically, freer to play games with the first-person speaker of their poems than those who must offer themselves to a wider readership, since the recipients are aware of the 'real' poet, and need not anxiously decode the text in pursuit of irony or distance. Second, the freedom for play that this offers suits an aristocratic code, with its high valuation of a chameleon-like *sprezzatura* that can slip readily from role to role. Third, it means that the emphasis of such poetry is much less upon the declaration of self, much more upon the exhibition of an artful mastery of language and idea.

Philip Sidney's *Astrophil and Stella* demonstrates these points excellently. The identification of the poet–speaker, Astrophil, with the historical Sidney is invited at many points in the sequence. Sonnets are built upon tournaments in which he took part, upon the coat of arms of the Sidney family and so on. Furthermore, several sonnets are simply incomprehensible if it is not known that the Stella to whom they are addressed is the historical personage Penelope Rich. So, to a certain extent, the now derided instinct of earlier critics to enquire into the historical reality of the relationship between Sidney and Penelope Rich is not entirely misplaced. What it mistakes, however, is the social context within which this fictional version of their relationship is played out. For though the first sonnet establishes the lady as the recipient of the poems, and therefore suggests that sincere declaration of feeling is the intention of the sequence, the real audience includes also those friends who, knowing the actual state of affairs, can be amused at the gaps they perceive between the fictional Astrophil and the real Philip Sidney and can therefore appreciate the craft that goes into the creation of self-as-lover.

In some ways, then, lyric poems such as these *are* 'personal', part of a real exchange between individuals, and it is quite wrong for the modern reader to whom those circumstances are irrecoverable in detail to ignore the significance of their existence for the nature of the presentation of the first-person speaker. But equally it is wrong to interpret sonnets as if they were transparent utterances declaring straightforwardly the 'real feelings' of the poet.

The self-conscious play of these sonnets – like the teasing of earnest Orlando by Rosalind in *As You Like It* – makes the language of love and the conventional attitudes of the lover into problems to be debated, and their correspondence to reality into a subject of enquiry.

The appeal of Donne's poetry to Eliot and others at the beginning of this century rested in no small measure upon the fact that his speaker is not to be read as projecting the 'feelings' of John Donne in any direct fashion, but rather as a series of masks which permitted him to explore ideas, literary conventions and diction. Even more than in the sonnets of Sidney or Shakespeare (though no differently from many other sonnet sequences) the speaker is dramatically created.

Though probably few students would nowadays attempt to read

the *Songs and Sonets* as 'sincere' Romantic lyrics, it is still true that many resist the full implication of their play with literary convention or the fictiveness of their speaker. So, for example, the wit of a poem like 'The Apparition' depends upon the reader's recognition of its subversion of a number of standard sonneteering motifs – the lover 'dying' of grief; the virginal idealized lady; the dream of the beloved – in a form which is a kind of deformed sonnet, to make up a lyric which itself belongs in the convention called by Cairns the 'threat prophecy'. 'The Good Morrow' is often taken as if it were a straightforward celebration of 'Donne's' vision of a perfect fusion in love. To do so is to neglect the way the poem, like the sonnets of Sidney, is a rhetorical attempt to persuade the woman to whom it is addressed of the sincerity of the speaker's passion, an attempt from which we as readers are invited to distance ourselves. The complacency of the ending of the first stanza:

> If ever any beauty I did see,
> Which I desired and got, 'twas but a dream of thee
>
> (ll. 6–7)

leaves open the question whether the ensuing declaration of love is not just the patter that this lover dishes out to any beauty on the morning after the night before.

There is, however, an important distinction to be made between the fictional personae of Sidney and of Donne. Where Sidney invites us to measure the fictionality of his speaker against a real identity known to his original readers, Donne (at least as far as we can now tell) inscribes the possibility of dramatizing his speakers within the lyrics themselves. Hence, possibly, the attraction of Donne for critics of the 'Verbal Icon' school, to whom the ultimately more difficult and intractable ironies of Sidney were much less attractive.

Towards the end of this period, however, there are signs of a shift in attitude to the business and role of the poet that is to have considerable significance in the later evolution of the lyric 'I'. One important factor in the change is the emergence of the professional poet looking towards publication as his goal, and claiming a high

dignity for his craft with none of the amateur modesty of an aristo-
crat such as Sidney.

Ben Jonson is one such figure. Interestingly, and characteristically, most of his poetic energy goes into genres like epigram and
epistle, or into the most public of lyric kinds, the ode. For him the
high calling of poetry depended upon the integrity of its practitioners, and therefore upon an identity between the poet and the
'I' his poems deploy. ('I mean what I say,' he declared in 'Epistle
to Master John Selden'.) He was, of course, capable of writing love
lyrics of a conventional kind (including the fine, exultant 'See the
chariot at hand here of love'), but he also includes in his poem 'My
picture left in Scotland' a memorable and accurate self-portrait:

> Oh, but my conscious fears,
>   That fly my thoughts between,
>   Tell me that she hath seen
> My hundreds of grey hairs,
> Told seven and forty years,
> Read so much waist, as she cannot embrace
> My mountain belly and my rocky face,
> And all these through her eyes, have stopped her ears.

(ll. 10–18)

But though this is true to the facts of Jonson's appearance and age,
and may even have corresponded to some autobiographical reality,
the poem as a whole is cast as a witty extension of the opening
proposition, 'I now think, Love is rather deaf, than blind', and is
therefore quite different in character from Romantic lyrics of self-
exploration.

Michael Drayton in many ways seems, though a professional
writer, to inhabit an older world. His dedication of the *Odes* has
this to say:

> Beleeve it, he must have the Trick
> Of Ryming, with Invention quick,
>   That should doe *Lyricks* well.

(ll. 7–9)

But in addressing the reader of his sonnet sequence *Idea* he differentiates himself from the conventional whining lover, saying:

> My Verse is the true image of my Mind,
> Ever in motion, still desiring change;
> And as thus to Varietie inclin'd
> So in all Humors sportively I range.
>
> ('To the Reader of These Sonnets', ll. 9–12)

As has earlier been said, the emphasis on lyric poetry as image of the poet's mind is a very important aspect of the transformation and internalization of the ode during the eighteenth century. But it would be wrong to read back into Drayton and the Renaissance lyric in general attitudes that crystallized in Romantic aesthetic theory. Underlying Drayton's assertion are the recommendations of rhetoricians like Puttenham, who suggested that love poetry should be 'variable, inconstant, affected, curious and most witty of any others', because 'love is of all other humane affections the most puissant and passionate, and most generall to all sortes and ages of men and women' (*The Arte of English Poesie*, 1589, p. 36). It is the job of the lyric poet to image the postures of the lover by his deployment of the arts of language. The fundamentally rhetorical nature of Renaissance lyric is represented in Sidney's comments on his contemporary love poets in *An Apology for Poetry*:

> But truly many of such writings as come under the banner of unresistible love, if I were a mistress, would never persuade me they were in love; so coldly they apply fiery speeches, as men that had rather read lovers' writings . . . than that in truth they feel those passions, which easily (as I think) may be betrayed by that same forcibleness or *energia* (as the Greeks call it) of the writer.
>
> (Geoffrey Shepherd (ed.), London, 1965, pp. 137–8)

Two points are worth noting. First, Sidney as reader casts himself in the role of the mistress who is to be *persuaded* by the poetry.

Renaissance lyric is rarely, if ever, the voice 'talking to itself or to nobody'. It is always a directed performance. Second, the very chain of this complex sentence seems to indicate the ambivalent status of the 'I' in Renaissance lyric. It begins with 'writings' as its subject as if to declare the self-consciously rhetorical and fictional status of the speaker, but ends with the writer – characterized by rhetorical energy, but displaying his arts in the cause of 'truth'.

On the one side there is the aristocratic amateur, known to his initial audience, sporting with the teasing relationship of author and persona. His poetry circulated in manuscript, and in the process became detached from the 'author', and amenable to recomposition by anyone who chose to transcribe it into a commonplace book. On the other side there is the increasingly professional poet, publishing his works, claiming their authorship and censorious of imperfect or 'stolen' versions. For him, increasingly, 'integrity' becomes a central virtue, and an identity of poet and persona is claimed more frequently.

This, of course, is a very simplified picture, and does not claim in any way to bring to the surface all the cultural conditions of which this transformation might be held to be symptomatic. But before leaving the Renaissance, it is instructive to look very briefly at the rather special case of the religious lyric.

For though, as we have seen, there are a number of kinds of religious lyric, and poets could employ narrative, or place words in the mouth of Christ, Mary or Magdalene, or else act as spokesmen for the people of God in hymns of praise; when they turned inward and presented a picture of themselves they were forbidden the resources of irony. A religious poet must always seem to mean what he says. Furthermore, though he, like the secular sonneteer, writes with a sense of an audience, albeit an audience he wishes to instruct rather than to amuse, he speaks, not to the fictional construct of the idealized lady, but to the God whom he believes knows all he can say before he says it. The lyric 'Overheard by God' (to use the title of A. D. Nuttall's book on the subject (London, 1980)) poses peculiar problems of tact.

Christianity emphasizes the importance of the individual's spiritual experience, but demands the suppression of the ego in the knowledge of God's all-pervading grace. When Donne speaks to God with the same urgency as he does to his mistresses, but without the defence of fiction, his words can seem too hubristic. Crashaw's baroque fantasias seem, at least to more recent taste, self-regarding in their verbal density. For though ceremonious and elaborate language may be appropriate in the poetry of praise from Dunbar to Hopkins, the inwardness of spiritual experience either reaches beyond speech or else records only the beating upon the cloud of unknowing.

George Herbert resolved some of these dilemmas by a number of overlapping strategies. His lyrics, though intended to 'find / Him who a sermon flies', frequently deal directly with personal spiritual experience. He rejects ornament, and the verses that are 'too fine a thing' for his 'rough sorrows' ('Grief'). But, at the same time, he draws attention to the artistry of his poetry, in shaped poems like 'Easter Wings', for example, or in the opening stanza of 'Deniall':

> When my devotions could not pierce
> > Thy silent eares;
> Then was my heart broken, as was my verse:
> > My breast was full of feares
> > > And disorder.

(ll. 1–5)

But the display of contrivance in a poem like this (which 'mends' the rhyme of the final line in the last stanza) is, paradoxically, a means of diverting attention from the first-person speaker as it turns the poem into an icon (or 'hieroglyph' in Joseph Summers's term (*George Herbert*, London, 1954)). It becomes available to every Christian reader as a meditative object. Furthermore this poem stands before 'Christmas' in *The Temple*, and, by its recalling of the Advent prayer, '*Come, come, my God O come*', places the individual's experience of God's absence into the larger context of the Church's seasonal patterns. Elsewhere Herbert comes to an understanding of his personal spiritual plight by seeing it as typologically reflecting biblical narrative.

In the two sonnets 'The Holy Scriptures' Herbert explores the relationship of the individual Christian's life to Scriptural story. They are fascinating statements about the business of reading – whether of sacred or secular texts – but they also indicate how Herbert deflects egocentricity even as he deals with the most inward of spiritual experience. He writes:

> Such are thy secrets, which my life makes good,
>   And comments on thee: for in ev'ry thing
>   Thy words do finde me out, and parallels bring,
> And in another make me understood.
>
> ('The Holy Scriptures II', ll. 9–12)

What Herbert is attempting, then, is not a poetry whose *language* is 'transparent', giving access to the speaking self of the poet. Instead he struggles to make the 'self' of the poetry transparent; to become, like the preacher of 'The Windows', 'a window' in which God 'anneals' his story.

It is often assumed that from the late seventeenth century until the end of the eighteenth, lyric went to sleep. 'Satire flourishes while lyric all but disappears; confession is replaced by autobiography' as the introduction to one influential anthology states (Geoffrey Tillotson, Paul Fussell and Marshall Waingrow (eds), *Eighteenth Century Literature*, New York, 1969, p. 4).

There is, no doubt, some truth in this observation. But it tells us at least as much about modern generic assumptions as it does about eighteenth-century literature. It is not so much that lyric disappears, as that the tendency of post-Romantic readers to assume that lyric is personal and private renders much of the poetry of the period invisible. Various reasons might be adduced for the absence of intensely personal lyric in the period – the influence of Locke's philosophy; the condition of writers aiming at a large audience in print, but not yet wholly free of the system of patronage; the pressure of neo-classicism which tends to shift the focus from the deeply personal – and so on.

But, of course, lyric can properly be regarded as a public and social genre. Akenside's 'Ode on Lyric Poetry' invokes the same classical authors as Drayton in his earlier quoted preface, and imagines their inspiration visiting him:

> When friendship and when lettered mirth
> Haply partake my simple board.

(ll. 101–2)

This is the kind of context in which the innumerable love lyrics, with their Chloes, Chlorindas and the rest, must be placed. The point here is a simple one – there are many, many lyrics written in the period, from broadside ballad to the pastoral lyrics favoured by serious composers. Most of them, no doubt, like the mass-produced songs of more recent ages, repeat platitudes and endorse social convention. There are exceptions, from 'The Vicar of Bray' to Cowper's telling attack on slavery in 'The Negro's Complaint' (Davie, *Augustan Lyric*, London, 1974, pp. 122–3), where the public and social function of the lyric is given satiric point. In the main, however, as Mark Booth makes clear in *The Experience of Songs*, these lyrics are not amenable to the kinds of discussion which privilege the complexity of 'literary' lyric, and demand a critical attention of a more sociological kind if they are to yield rewards to the contemporary reader.

The 'I' of these lyrics is largely conventional, a persona which allows the poem to be readily and immediately appropriated by each member of its audience. The same is true of most of the religious lyrics of the period, the hymns for which Donald Davie argues so forcibly in *Purity of Diction in English Poetry* and in the introduction to *Augustan Lyric*. Booth analyses excellently the way Wesley's 'Come down O love divine' 'works by drawing its human congregation into some level of communion transcending self' (op. cit., p. 135). There can be no room in hymns for detail that predicates a personal life of the poet outside the poem, or interferes with the capacity of any individual reader to make the poem his own.

The way these lyrics are immediately generalizable fits with the prescription Johnson's Imlac offers in *Rasselas*:

> The business of a poet . . . is to examine, not the individual, but the species; to remark general properties and large appearances: he does not number the streaks of the tulip, or describe the different shades in the verdure of the forest. He is to exhibit in his portraits of nature such prominent and striking features, as recall the original to every mind; and must neglect the minuter discriminations, which one may have remarked, and another have neglected.
>
> (Chapter X)

Shortly afterwards the poet is told to 'disregard present laws and opinions, and rise to general and transcendental truths, which will always be the same'.

These assumptions lie behind Johnson's distaste for the metaphysical poets, who never attain the 'grandeur of generality', and similarly behind his praise for Gray's *Elegy*, which 'abounds with images to which every bosom returns an echo'. They would certainly seem to militate against the exploration of the poet's interior and private world. But in any case, for Johnson, as his comments in the *Life of Shenstone* indicate, it is the elegy which serves as the vehicle for 'the effusion of a contemplative mind', whereas lyrics are to be divided, as they had been for Drayton, into the lighter kinds, for which 'ease and airiness' are appropriate, or the grander ode, which demands 'vehemence and elevation'.

As has already been suggested, the elegiac modulation of the lyric is one important ingredient in its transformation into the interiority that now seems such an important aspect of its generic definition. Coleridge's remarks in *Table Talk* make this clear:

> Elegy is the form of poetry natural to the reflective mind. It *may* treat of any subject, but it must treat of no subject for *itself*,

but always and exclusively with reference to the poet himself. As he will feel regret for the past or desire for the future, so sorrow and love become the principal themes of elegy.

(T. Ashe (ed.), London, 1923, p. 263)

In the development of the ode, the sublimity of its diction is seen increasingly as a mark of the imaginative power of the poet, rather than as a tribute to the sublimity of its subject.

Modulations such as these are not causes of the changes in poetic theory at the end of the eighteenth century. They witness to the poets' growing sense of alienation from the urban, materialist world and the retreat to the solitary world of the mind; to the erosion of stable religious, social and political belief; to the profound alteration in the range and scope of poetry's world effected by the growth of the novel and so on. Shelley's effort in *A Defence of Poetry* to claim that 'poetry is indeed something divine' does not in the end get round Peacock's observation in *The Four Ages of Poetry* that poetry 'takes its rise in the demand for the commodity, and flourishes in proportion to the extent of the market' (H. F. B. Brett-Smith (ed.), Oxford, 1972, p. 4). Indeed it can be argued that the inwardness of much Romantic poetry is precisely an attempt to cope with the tensions that these two statements articulate.

Romantics, as much as Johnson, desired that their poetry should articulate truths available to all. Wordsworth argued, in the revised version of the *Preface to the Lyrical Ballads*, that 'Poetry is the most philosophic of all writing . . . its object is truth, not individual and local, but general and operative' (R. L. Brett and A. R. Jones (eds), revised edn, London, 1965, p. 257). Keats in a letter to John Taylor asserted:

> In poetry I have a few Axioms, and you will see how far I am from their Centre. First I think Poetry should surprise by a fine excess and not by Singularity – it should strike the reader as a wording of his own highest thoughts, and appear almost a Remembrance.
>
> (Robert Gittings (ed.), *Letters*, Oxford, 1970, p. 69)

But for Romantic poets this general truth is to be attained by truth to specifics. Blake claimed that 'Single and particular detail is the foundation of the Sublime.' Moreover, the true subject of poetry is not the objective world outside, but the poet's imaginative faculty which has the capacity to heal 'the cleavage between the subject and object, between the vital, purposeful, value-full world of private experience and the dead postulated world of extension, quantity and motion' (Abrams, *The Mirror and the Lamp*, p. 65).

But though subjectivity is the condition of most Romantic poetry, it is far too simple to seize on Wordsworth's famous tag: 'Poetry is the spontaneous overflow of powerful feelings' (*Preface to the Lyrical Ballads*, p. 246), and to read the 'I' of Romantic lyric as if it is merely to be identified with the poet – however much one might be encouraged to do so by Keats's attack on Wordsworth's 'egotistical sublime' (Gittings, op. cit., p. 157), or Byron's scathing dismissal of Keats:

> such writing is a sort of mental masturbation. . . . I don't mean he is *indecent*, but viciously soliciting his own ideas into a state, which is neither poetry nor any thing but a Bedlam vision produced by raw pork and onion.
>
> (Peter Gunn (ed.), *Lord Byron: Selected Prose*, Harmondsworth, 1972, p. 357)

The exploration of the self and its relation to the world demands that all kinds of literary strategies be employed, including, as Robert Langbaum's study, *The Poetry of Experience* (New York, 1963), demonstrates, the play between dramatic and personal genres.

So, for example, Blake's idiosyncratic vision is couched, in *The Songs of Innocence and Experience* at least, within a presentation of the first-person speaker that is apparently quite traditional. Lyrics use dramatic speakers ('The Chimney Sweep'), or detached, emblematic speech ('O Rose, thou art sick'), and even when the 'I' is more 'personal', it offers itself to the reader as speaking, like the 'I' of Watts or Wesley, for a collective awareness, even though the things it sees, in 'London', for example, are very different from the pieties of hymnody. The large-scale strategy of the collection is to undermine the security of these conventional personae, to point to their inadequacy.

The collection *Lyrical Ballads* implies, in its very title, a tension between narrative and personal feeling (increasingly, and historically for the first time, identified with 'lyric'). Wordsworth employs a wide variety of strategies to trace 'the fluxes and refluxes of the mind'. The three Lucy poems culminate in the exquisite 'A slumber did my spirit seal', whose speaker is 'personal', but not individualized or private. Coleridge did not know whether there was any 'real' Lucy, and all subsequent attempts to find one are even more misplaced than the pursuit of Shakespeare's 'young man right fair', since the poem does not gesture outside itself. 'The Thorn', and many other of the ballads, employ fully dramatic speakers, as Wordsworth himself was anxious to point out. More complex is the strategy of a poem like 'Hart-Leap Well', which opens as an apparently straightforward narrative, but then, in the second part, is revealed as a story spoken to the poet by a shepherd, a story that perhaps accounts for the present state of the place the poet contemplates, and from it a moral is drawn. The reader of this poem is involved in the revaluation of the narrative he has read. In 'There was a Boy' (at least as it stands in this collection – it was later incorporated in *The Prelude*) the reader is engaged in a more complex process of decoding. It begins as if it were a narrative, but ends with the picture of the mute poet standing by the boy's grave. We begin to understand that the boy is a figure for the poet himself, the poem an effort to speak the former experiences that time has taken away from the now dumb poet. 'Nutting' approaches the same sort of experience in a more open and direct way. The first-person speaker is clearly situated – as one recounting a past and personal story. That story is established precisely by the gap between the 'now' of the poem's composition and the 'then' of the experience it records. It is 'emotion recollected in tranquillity', but at the same time registers uncertainty about the accuracy of that recollection.

roems like 'Nutting' and 'Hart-Leap Well' represent significan
extension of the lyric territory into meditation upon a narrative
either from the poet's 'own' past or from a book. (Arnold's 'Schola
Gipsy' is an example of the latter, Frost's 'After Apple-Picking' o
the former.) The 'then–now' strategy enables the potentia
openness of narrative to be contained and given significance by an
within the projected consciousness of the poem's speaker. It als
suits well with the pervasive elegiac note of much lyric poetry of th
nineteenth century, and figures the sense that the poet's business is
in Shelley's words, to 'arrest the vanishing apparitions which haun
the interlunations of life'. 'Poetry redeems from decay the visi
tations of the divinity in man,' he asserts (H. F. B. Brett-Smith (ed.)
A Defence of Poetry, Oxford, 1972, p. 55). It is the urgency of tha
desire, and the sense of the precariousness of its achievement, that i
figured in the transformations of narrative into lyric 'spots of time
in so many Romantic and subsequent poems. (It should, however
be stressed that the notion of lyric as being defined by its dealin
with atemporal moments of illumination is one that takes shap
precisely under the pressure of this Romantic aesthetic. It was *not* a
necessary condition of earlier lyric poetry.)

The exploration of self and subjectivity by projection int
narratively realized figures is one lyric strategy. In the 'greate
lyric', the ode, the poets seem to be speaking directly in their ow
voice, and addressing their speech to Autumn, the West Wind, th
Nightingale and so on. The attempt is often to capture a transcen
dent moment when the poet can feel himself transported and full
identified with the object of his meditations. Shelley pleads:

> Make me thy lyre, even as the forest is:
> What if my leaves are falling like its own!
> The tumult of thy mighty harmonies
>
> Will take from both a deep, autumnal tone,
> Sweet though in Sadness. Be thou, Spirit fierce,
> My spirit! Be thou me, impetuous one!
>
> ('Ode to the West Wind', ll. 57–62)

But the visions are fragile. Keats, raised to enthusiasm by the song of the nightingale, returns from rapture:

> Forlorn! the very word is like a bell
>   To toll me back from thee to my sole self!
> Adieu! the fancy cannot cheat so well
>   As she is famed to do, deceiving elf.
>
> ('Ode to a Nightingale', ll. 71–4)

In an obvious way this poem requires us as readers to 'identify' ourselves with the poet–speaker of the poem, who has established his presence by the narrative particularity with which the poem opens. The transition achieved by the word 'forlorn', however, invites us to see the maker of words at work, to recognize the 'fictiveness' of the poem's discourse. This, as Culler shows, is true also of the apostrophic nature of the address of most of the great odes:

> If, as we tend to assume, post-enlightenment poetry seeks to overcome the alienation of subject from object, then apostrophe takes the crucial step of constituting the object as another subject with whom the poetic subject might hope to strike up a harmonious relationship. Apostrophe would figure this reconciliation of subject and object. But one must note that it figures this reconciliation as an act of will, as something to be accomplished poetically in the act of apostrophising; and apostrophic poems display in various ways awareness of the difficulties of what they purport to speak.
>
> (*The Pursuit of Signs*, p. 143)

The major point to be recognized here is that, even as Romantic poetry places the poet's subjective consciousness firmly at the centre, and thus asks us to take the 'I' as directly expressing the feelings of the poet in the way which has come to seem prescriptive for the lyric, in various ways it also requires us to recognize the problems that derive from that identification.

There are countless lyrics where the fictiveness of poetic dis course is minimized. Byron's 'On This Day I Complete My Thirty-Sixth Year' is one such poem – looking back to Milton' 'Sonnet VII', which begins 'How soon hath time the subtle thief o youth, / Stol'n on his wing my three and twentieth year', and forward to a considerable number of lyrics, of which Blunden': 'Report on Experience' and Roy Fuller's 'On His Sixty-Fifth Birthday' are examples. So too John Clare's despairing 'I am', would somehow lose its power if we were to learn that the poet wa: not shut up in an asylum, but a contented socialite.

The 'somehow' in that last sentence, however, marks an import ant fact. The identification of poet and persona, the requiremen for a lyric to speak the personal feelings of the poet is as much the product of the desire of readers as it is of the purposes of poets o even of the nature of texts. The contract we make with a poem i: determined by prevailing attitudes, the ways we gain access to poems, the ways that criticism finds to talk about them.

Shelley's statement 'All things exist as they are perceived; a least in relation to the percipient' is central to the poetics o Romanticism. He was confident that 'poetry defeats the curse which binds us to be subjected to the accident of surrounding impressions' (Brett-Smith, op. cit., p. 56). The subsequent history of lyric poetry down to the present day might be seen as exploring the premise, and doubting the conclusion.

The ebbing of the 'sea of faith' in the Victorian period put increasing pressure on poetry to fulfil a quasi-religious function in the face of an increasingly meaningless world. Arnold's 'Dover Beach' is a classic expression of the mood:

> Ah love, let us be true
> To one another! for the world, which seems
> To lie before us like a land of dreams,
> So various, so beautiful, so new,
> Hath really neither joy, nor love, nor light,
> Nor certitude, nor peace, nor help for pain;

And we are here as on a darkling plain
Swept with confused alarms of struggle and flight,
Where ignorant armies clash by night.

(ll. 29–37)

(Though one should note the appeal to human love as a sanctuary – an important extension of Romantic solipsism, as Pat Ball shows in *The Heart's Events*, London, 1976.)

Tennyson's recasting of the Wordsworthian vision of childhood in *In Memoriam XLV* betokens a deep sense of self as prison:

So rounds he to a separate mind
From whence clear memory may begin,
As through the frame that binds him in
His isolation grows defined.

(ll. 9–12)

Victorian lyric largely operates within the parameters set out by the Romantics, and most poems are sustained by their presentation of the individual 'I', whose words are to be trusted and interpreted by the reader as the representation of the poet's thoughts and feelings. Towards the end of the century, however, the growth of 'aestheticism', with its slogan 'art for art's sake', and the parallel symbolist movement in France, developing a doctrine of the estranged poet's truth to the transcendent image, were to be of enormous significance for the generation of poets we know as the modernists, as Frank Kermode amply demonstrates in *Romantic Image* (London, 1957).

At one level the poets of the early decades of this century needed to react against, and make new, the inheritance of late-Victorian poetry and its Georgian mutant. Their extension of subject-matter to take in the facts of urban life; their effort to find a poetic language that might accurately and truthfully present the poet's vision, whether the idiosyncratic speech of Hopkins or the pared-down language of the imagist enterprise, can both be seen as enacting an inevitable process in the history of poetry.

The demand to 'make it new' will often involve a reaction against immediate predecessors and a concomitant resurrection of some past generation. Eliot's attention to the metaphysicals is well known (even if it was not as original to him as once was supposed). Donald Davie wrote *Purity of Diction*, rehabilitating eighteenth-century poets, as a manifesto for the writers of the 1950s who needed to escape the pervasive influence of Eliot and modernism. Of course the relationship of the poet to the past is extremely complex – and in Harold Bloom's *The Anxiety of Influence* (New York, 1973) and subsequent writings, or John Hollander's *The Figure of Echo* (Berkeley and London, 1981), is subtly explored. Certainly one of the problems for the reader of contemporary lyric is that the range of reference to, or invocation of, other literatures is far wider than it would have been in earlier centuries. But just as the relationship with classical literature in the eighteenth century could be endured, celebrated or exploited in a variety of ways, so modern poets may call up ghosts of the past for any number of different reasons.

Eliot in *The Wasteland* shores the fragments of the past against the ruined culture of the present. Auden invokes 'Chaucer, Langland, Douglas, Dunbar' in his 'Ode to the Medieval Poets' as a happy contrast to modern makers, only to find that their presence disables him from writing 'verses to applaud a thundery / jovial June'. In the tenth of Seamus Heaney's 'Glanmore Sonnets', from *Field Work*, a dream is recounted. In the octave 'we' sleep outside, 'laid out / like breathing effigies on a raised ground'. The sestet sets against this image a memory expressed in recollection of Wyatt's 'They flee from me':

> And in that dream I dreamt – how like you this? –
> Our first night years ago in that hotel
> When you came with your deliberate kiss
> To raise us towards the lovely and painful
> Covenants of flesh;

(ll. 9–13)

The act of recollecting a literary 'ghost' figures the wistful memory of an earlier state in their relationship, and seems to perform a curative function. Very different is the viciously ironic recasting of the same Wyatt original in Gavin Ewart's 'They flee from me':

> At this moment in time
> the chicks that went for me
> in a big way
> are opting out;
> as of now, it's an all change situation.
>
> (ll. 1–5, in D. J. Enright (ed.), *The Oxford Book of Contemporary Verse*, Oxford, 1980, p. 77)

It is a caustic lament for the corruption of language, and, in its deployment of free verse a savage comment on the tendency of certain contemporary poetic schools.

One could extend examples and kinds of recollection infinitely. The larger point is a simple but important one. The poetry of this century needs to be understood in the light of its past which it may recollect or disown, but cannot escape. So modernism, for all its apparent discontinuity with its Romantic antecedent, and the 'isms' that have in turn displaced it, can usefully, if rather crudely, be seen as working through problems implicit in Romantic theory and practice.

Put at its simplest the Romantic lyric declares 'I, the poet, feel or understand something in relation to an object.' If, however, as Shelley declared in *A Defence of Poetry*, 'All things exist as they are perceived; at least in relation to the percipient,' then the danger of solipsism looms, for how can the reader be persuaded to accept that things are as the poet sees them? One answer is to trust the magisterial 'I' of the poem, which declares, as Whitman put it:

> I celebrate myself, and sing myself,
> And what I assume you shall assume,
> For every atom belonging to me as good belongs to you.
>
> ('Song of Myself', ll. 1–3)

But what if the 'I' is to be trusted as little as objective reality; if, as Keats claimed, the 'chameleon poet' has 'no self'? The answer then must be for the reader to trust the poem as an object with an elusive relationship both to poet and to external reality. But, as has increasingly been recognized in this century, the language of which poems are made is itself fundamentally slippery and unstable. The problems these layers of uncertainty give rise to has been the subject of most poetic theory in this century. Robert Pinsky in his book *The Situation of Poetry* (Princeton, 1976) suggests:

> This uneasy relation with one's own medium has led Romantic and post-Romantic poets to devise remarkable ways of writing, which might make language seem less abstract and less discursive. The Poem has pursued the condition of a thing.
>
> (p. 58)

It is impossible to do more than sketch some of the strategies of that pursuit. For Eliot and other modernist poets, the use of masks or personae seemed to be one way out of the dilemma of subjectivity. Fernando Pessoa, indeed, wrote poetry of four quite distinct kinds under four different names. The difficulty is, however, that the reader faced by the collected works of a poet will still rehabilitate the supervisory personality of the poet as it is refracted to him through the masks of J. Alfred Prufrock, Tiresias, Gerontion and the rest.

Eliot's anti-subjective manifesto was offered in the essay 'Tradition and the Individual Talent', where he declared: 'Poetry is not the expression of personality but an escape from personality.' In so far as this means that it is inappropriate to read Eliot's poetry as if it were simply confessional it is significant, but the sting comes in the continuation: 'But of course, only those who have personality and emotions know what it means to want to escape from these things' (*Selected Essays*, p. 21). What Eliot's poetry now seems to record is precisely that 'want', that symbolist effort to achieve the transcendent image, which yet, as Kermode argues, predicates the isolated figure of the poet who can perceive it.

Pound, in a letter to Harriet Monroe reprinted in Peter Jones's anthology, *Imagist Poetry*, urged: 'Objectivity and again objectivity, and expression' (op. cit., p. 133). But the hard-edged isolated image presented in a poem still leaves the reader asking who said it, and why. We still want to recuperate the images by relating them back to the poet who conceived them. It is indeed interesting that among those who claim descent from Pound are William Carlos Williams with his battle cry 'no poetry but in things', and the projectivist manifesto of Olson which speaks of 'the getting rid of the interference of the individual as ego'. But at the same time surrealism has drawn upon imagist technique and Freudian psychology to explore the depths of personality locked in the subconscious, and has had considerable effect upon the practice of poets called 'confessional'.

Wallace Stevens probed continuously throughout his poetic career at the vexed relationship between imagination and reality. He wrote: 'The subject-matter of poetry is not that "collection of solid, static objects extended in space" but the life that is lived in the scene that it composes' (Scully, op. cit., p. 144). He essayed 'Thirteen Ways of Looking at a Blackbird', teased language to the edge of nonsense, but ultimately asserted the power of art to order that which surrounds it, in poems like 'Anecdote of a Jar' and 'The Idea of Order at Key West', which concludes:

> Oh! Blessed rage for order, pale Ramon,
> The maker's rage to order words of the sea,
> Words of the fragrant portals, dimly-starred,
> And of ourselves and of our origins,
> In ghostlier demarcations, keener sounds.

(ll. 52–6)

Again, the ego of the poet is deflected, lyrics offer themselves as transcending mere subjectivism as they trace the reciprocal play of perceiver and perceived, and recognize the slipperiness of language, but ultimately the 'maker' stands before us. His responsibility is to his readers, and his function 'to make his imagination theirs'.

In the battlegrounds of the various schools of contemporary lyric the problems of subjectivity versus objectivity, the position of the poet in relation to the 'I' of the lyric, to the reader and to objective reality have been endlessly debated.

One 'front' in the battle has been the question of form. Yeats said:

> If I wrote of personal love or sorrow in free verse, or in any rhythm that left it unchanged, amid all its accidence, I would be full of self-contempt because of my egotism and indiscretion, and foresee the boredom of my reader. I must choose a traditional stanza, even what I alter must seem traditional.
>
> (Scully, op. cit., p. 24)

The sense of the form of the poem as 'contraption' was vital to Auden, who said in one of his 'Shorts':

> Blessed be all metrical rules that forbid automatic responses,
>   force us to have second thoughts, free from the fetters of Self.

Craft can turn the poem into an object seemingly independent of its writer as a subjective individual. The poets of the mid-century, taking their cue from Auden and looking back often to the poetry of the Renaissance, explored the distancing possibilities of wit and verbal play. Richard Wilbur and early Lowell are American examples; John Fuller a contemporary scion of the stock. The dangers of this manner are a decorative aridity, an empty triviality.

Free verse, by contrast, seems to allow for a direct presentation of the speaking voice of the poet. The influence of Whitman on contemporary American poets has been of great significance. A 'performance poet' like Allen Ginsberg, committed to the illusion of spontaneous improvisation, seems exultantly to project his own personality, his own voice, with no attempt at deflection. But though free verse can often seem to be merely a way of permitting a rampant subjectivism back into poetry, it has also served, in the poetry of William Carlos Williams and his descendants, a slightly different end. The rejection of traditional verse-patterns frees the poet for direct treatment of the thing, and enables the poet to present the way one perception leads to another with the urgency Olson demanded:

> if you also set up as a poet, USE USE USE the process at all points, in any given poem always, always one perception must must must MOVE, INSTANTER, ON ANOTHER.
>
> (Scully, op. cit., p. 273)

The controlling ego of the poet is therefore to be abolished as he presents the 'spontaneous overflow' of feeling, without the fixing in a frame that the 'recollection in tranquillity' implies.

Despite the efforts of various schools to blot out the 'lyrical ego', the latter part of this century has seen its reintroduction, albeit in very different ways. One reason for the relief with which many readers come to the poetry of Philip Larkin or Seamus Heaney is precisely that their affiliation to Hardy or to Wordsworth seems to permit a relatively unproblematic recuperation of their lyric 'I'. The figure in 'Church Going' who removes his cycle clips is clearly a representation of Larkin – or at least of the public persona he has created – and his meditation upon the church at which he has stopped and his response to it seems very traditional in its procedure. So too does Heaney's manifesto in his essay 'Feeling into Words', which begins with a quotation from *The Prelude*, and continues:

> Implicit in those lines is a view of poetry which I think is implicit in the few poems I have written that give me any right to speak: poetry as divination, poetry as revelation of the self to the self, as restoration of the culture to itself.
>
> (*Preoccupations*, London, 1980, p. 41)

This is not to suggest that there is no obliqueness in the 'I' of Heaney's poetry, nor that he does not use strategies of dramatic speech, or techniques of distancing – but they are all comprehensible within the lyric tradition stretching back to the Romantics and beyond.

The poetry of the American 'confessional' school (however inadequate that label is for the poetry of later Lowell, Anne Sexton, Sylvia Plath, among others) is much more strenuous. Their excoriating self-examination tries to get below the conscious ego to the Freudian subconscious, using a strange, idiosyncratic and complex imagery. Confessional poetry can all too easily degenerate into a sloppy indulgence of self: its apparent irrationality may be less a struggle to comprehend than an excuse for exhibitionism. Nevertheless, the effort of the poets of the 1960s remains a significant departure from the impersonality of modernism.

Most twentieth-century lyric poetry, then, engages with the problematic nature of the standard definition which sees lyric as the expression of a poet's personal feelings. Surrealist poetry, or at least its descendants in the work of John Ashbery and his followers, takes this assault one stage further. For, as we have seen, most twentieth-century poetry, however complex, ultimately permits the reader to construct a single 'enunciative posture' (to recapitulate Culler's words) from which to view the poem. Virginia Forrest-Thompson describes an alternative procedure: 'Ashbery tells us nothing about who is writing the poem, or why, or in what world; he makes certain that we won't assume we know by using the disconnected image-complex . . . and he builds his structure on this' (*The Poetry of Artifice*, Manchester, 1978, pp. 157–8). Whether this is an exciting road, or a desperate dead-end, only time will tell. It is interesting that just as 'New Criticism', with its condemnation of the 'Intentional Fallacy' and its emphasis upon the poem as freestanding 'Verbal Icon', arose in response to modernism, so the current explosion of 'Deconstruction', which celebrates linguistic surface, denies presence, and affirms the undecidability of meaning, seems peculiarly fitted to provide a way of talking about *The Poetics of Indeterminacy* (to use the title of Marjorie Perloff's book (Princeton, 1981)).

This rapid tour of varieties of twentieth-century lyric is not intended to imply that the future lies necessarily with the last mentioned. There is life in the old humanism yet; poetry which engages directly with politics − though the efforts of the 1930s withered away − shows signs of revival, especially perhaps in the words-for-music of black communities. But the main question that the varieties of contemporary poetry raise is, in the context of this study: what use is the word 'lyric' as a term of discrimination?

Conclusion

The question raised at the end of the last chapter brings to the surface a tension that has been running throughout this brief study, the tension between a generic description that is historically particular to the lyric poems of specific periods, and the desire for a critical label which will be of general application.

The argument of the study has been, decidedly, that the only proper way to use the term 'lyric' is with precise historical awareness. The answer to the question must, therefore, be itself couched in 'historical' terms. 'Lyric' is, if at all, a useful label in the twentieth century only in terms of the kinds of critical discrimination we now find it necessary to make, and in relation to the whole apparatus of descriptive terms that our own culture employs.

At first sight it might seem that ours is a period in which all generic distinction is irretrievably blurred – including the distinction between prose and poetry. (Jonathan Holden, for example, in his book *The Rhetoric of Contemporary Lyric* (Bloomington, 1980) devotes one chapter to a discussion of 'The Prose Lyric'.) In this context 'lyric' has the air of a survivor from past systems, a discriminatory term with nothing much left to distinguish itself from. Yet, in practical terms, we still try to make distinctions between kinds of poems, still find it necessary to characterize parts of a poet's output, or to differentiate between different sorts of poets. For that effort the label 'lyric' still has a positive usefulness.

Part of the problem in our own period is that poetry itself now occupies a much smaller part of the literary landscape (and a less privileged position within it) than it once did. 'Lyric' is therefore often carelessly used to do duty for 'poetry' in general, contaminated by the way the modal adjective 'lyrical' has long slipped into standing for 'anything vaguely poetical'. The problems are further compounded by the fact that the long and varied history of the term presses upon its present use in two competing ways.

In the first place, the Romantic and post-Romantic definition of lyric by its 'radical of presentation' (to use Frye's terms) still carries significant force. Michael Hamburger, in his excellent survey of modern poetry, *The Truth of Poetry* (London, 1969), for example, writes: 'in lyrical poetry the semblance of necessity has always been created by a sense of emotional urgency, by the poet's personal involvement in the material of his art' (p. 312).

At the same time, the sense of lyric as being, in some more or less defined way, characterized by its connection with music has a persistent presence. So, for example, Ezra Pound distinguished two kinds of poetry:

> There is a sort of poetry where music, sheer melody, seems as if it were just bursting into speech. There is another sort of poetry where painting or sculpture seems as if it were 'just coming over into speech'.
>
> The first sort of poetry has long been called 'lyric'.
>
> (Peter Jones (ed.), *Imagist Poetry*, Harmondsworth, 1972, p. 21)

A third complication ensues because the very distinction which Pound makes has itself been eroded, partly under the pressure of the imagist movement, so that for many readers it is the presence of 'images' which is a defining feature of poetry itself, and therefore of the lyric. For them, Craig Raine's claim is paramount:

> images provide
>
> a kind of sustenance,
> alms for every beggared sense
>
> ('Shallots', *A Martian Sends a Postcard Home*,
> ll. 16–18)

These three qualities are not mutually exclusive, but none of them is sufficient of itself to define a poem as 'lyric', nor is the presence of all of them required in any one poem for it to be felt as belonging to the lyric genre.

In fact, there are three much simpler kinds of distinction that in practice we tend now to use. The first is the obvious separation out of words written to be set to music as 'lyrics' – though, as we have seen, this is not a particularly useful category in its predictive value for the kind of poetry included within it. The second is the much maligned criterion of brevity. Though, as was stated in the first section, this cannot be considered a universal criterion, it *is* one which has some force in present-day poetry. For a modern poet is unlikely to write a long poem which has the character of the 'epic', and long narratives of any kind are a rarity, prose having largely appropriated this demesne. Indeed any poem with narrative content is likely to have some of the personal qualities that in earlier times have been reserved for lyric. But we would want to distinguish Bunting's *Briggflats* or Williams's *Paterson*, or even Ashbery's 'Self-Portrait in a Convex Mirror', from poems of smaller scale. And, at the present moment, we do so in part by reserving the label 'lyric' for shorter poems (however we might want to call longer works, or parts of them, 'lyrical'). If we use 'lyric' to mark out shorter rather than longer poems, then it means that the descendants of the old 'Greater Lyric', such as the long rhapsodies of Ginsberg, are almost certainly not felt to belong in this category, but to need some other descriptive term.

The last simple category is that of formality. For while generic boundaries have indeed been much eroded, it has become true that the label tends to be reserved for poems which in one way or another gesture towards rhythmic organization, generally towards stanzaic form. Fragmentary poems, or poems which make the greater part of their impact visually, are not 'lyrics' in current usage.

Something of the way these simple criteria operate pragmatically can be seen if one considers Eliot's *Four Quartets*. Though they are very personal poems, one would not call them 'lyrics'. That label would, however, be bestowed unreservedly on the fourth section of each *Quartet* where stanza form and a fairly strict rhythmic pattern, sometimes allied with rhyme, are used in sections perhaps the least obviously personal in the poem. (It is perhaps worth observing that a contemporary ambition to write a longer work will tend to find expression in lyric sequences of one kind or another. Lowell and Berryman are characteristic practitioners.)

There is, however, more to it than this. For, as we have said, generic labels themselves are somewhat out of fashion in current critical language. So too, in our ironic age, poets fight shy of forms that seem too simple or conventions that seem to have become exhausted. In this context, 'lyric' carries with it a sense of belonging with the past, with things that could once be said, but can now be approached only with difficulty. Auden's 'Ode to the Medieval Poets' speaks of this disablement, and Norman MacCaig approaches the same problem in his wryly witty poem 'Gone are the Days', where he ironically contrasts a heroic past with the prosaic present, and concludes:

> So don't expect me, lady with no e
> to look at a lamb and feel lambkin
> or give me a down look because I bought
> my greaves and cuisses at Marks and Spencers.
>
> Pishtushery's out. But oh, how my heart swells
> to see you perched, perjink, on a bar stool,
> And though epics are shrunk into epigrams, let me
> buy a love potion, a gin, a double.

> (ll. 13–20)

A longing for a language of celebration, of straightforwardness, informs C. Day Lewis's *The Lyric Impulse*. Just as a modern composer would find it difficult to write a big tune in E-flat major, so the modern poet, he argues, can only approach the 'simple, sensuous and passionate' in an increasingly sidelong fashion. The ambition remains, in Denise Levertov's words, to find:

> Not 'common speech'
> a dead level
> but the uncommon speech of paradise,
> tongue in which oracles
> speak to beggars and pilgrims.

('A Common Ground', ll. 58–62)

But this ambition, which might properly be called 'lyric', is one that is difficult for the modern poet to attain, without slipping into the seemingly overblown or emptily rhetorical. (A difficulty Denise Levertov does not herself always circumvent.) What might be called the 'minimalist' response, of Robert Creeley for example, runs the opposite risk of seeming to demand of the reader a weighty response to apparently trivial material.

As Andrew Welsh's study *Roots of Lyric* reminds us, there are many poetic possibilities which the generic term holds, as it were, in suspension. Our own century, like those before it, reflects only some of those possibilities. Though any attempt to drive the word 'lyric' to a single precise significance would be doomed to failure, we can see that in the present poetic climate the term can and does function to differentiate some poems from others – those which are shorter and more formally controlled from longer or freer poems; those which in some way gesture towards past poetic possibility in either subject or diction or both, from those which are fully and fragmentarily espoused of the present. While many such poems do, in one way or another, present themselves as if being spoken by the poet himself, that is no longer a central criterion, as it was in the last century, though most modern lyrics do concentrate on a moment of insight or heightened perception.

There will, no doubt, be many arguments about particular cases, but no generic category is ever absolute, and all genres evolve through history. Our critical terminology, in its turn, evolves a few

paces behind the changing of poetic habit and style. What constitutes a lyric now is different from what did in the past, and from
what will in the future. As critics we can only attempt to be scru-
pulous in always using a generic term like 'lyric' with the fullest
possible historical awareness.

Select bibliography

This is not meant to be a comprehensive bibliography of the subject, nor even a complete listing of all titles cited in the course of the study. Instead, it aims to do no more than provide for students a small selection of titles that will enable them to go beyond the limits of this introductory work.

General genre theory

Cairns, Francis, *Generic Composition in Greek and Roman Poetry*, Edinburgh, Edinburgh University Press, 1972.

Colie, Rosalie L., *The Resources of Kind: Generic Theory in the Renaissance*, ed. Barbara K. Lewalski, Berkeley, University of California Press, 1973.

Especially good on ideas of generic 'blending' and the relationship between lyric and epigram.

Dubrow, Heather, *Genre*, London, Methuen, 1982.

Fowler, Alastair, *Kinds of Literature*, Oxford, Oxford University Press, 1982.

An ambitious and ample study, though one which resists the term 'lyric' as far as it can.

Frye, Northrop, *Anatomy of Criticism*, Princeton, Princeton University Press, 1957.

An influential and important work, defining lyric by its 'radical of presentation', and with some combative comments on the relationship of poetry and music.

Hernadi, Paul, *Beyond Genre*, Ithaca and London, Cornell University Press, 1972.

Wellek, René, 'Genre theory, the lyric and *Erlebnis*', in *Discriminations*, New Haven and London, Yale University Press, 1970. A devastating attack on the partitioning of literature into three, and upon expressionist theories of the lyric.

Wellek, René, and Warren, Austin, *Theory of Literature*, 3rd edn, New York, Harcourt, Brace & World, 1967.

On the lyric

Abrams, M. H., *The Mirror and The Lamp*, Oxford, Oxford University Press, 1953. A guide to the transformation of aesthetic theory in the Romantic period.

Abrams, M. H., 'Structure and style in the greater Romantic lyric', in *Romanticism and Consciousness*, ed. H. Bloom, New York, Norton, 1970.

Brower, Reuben A. (ed.), *Forms of Lyric*, New York and London, Columbia University Press, 1970.

Cameron, Sharon, *Lyric Time, Dickinson and the Limits of Genre*, Baltimore and London, Johns Hopkins Press, 1979. A difficult, but valuable book.

Culler, Jonathan, *Structuralist Poetics*, London, Routledge & Kegan Paul, 1975. Good on the way reader expectation defines genre.

Culler, Jonathan, 'Apostrophe', in *The Pursuit of Signs*, London, Routledge & Kegan Paul, 1981. One of the best applications of new critical approach to the subject.

Davie, Donald, *Purity of Diction in English Poetry*, London, Routledge & Kegan Paul, 1952. Especially good on the plain style and the didactic lyric.

Fuller, John, *The Sonnet*, London, Methuen, 1972.

Hardy, Barbara, *The Advantage of Lyric*, London, The Athlone Press, 1977.

Concentrates on the lyric as 'expression of feeling'.

Hollander, John, *Vision and Resonance*, New York, Oxford University Press, 1975.

Studies musical and visual aspects of poetry.

Jump, John, *The Ode*, London, Methuen, 1974.

Lewalski, Barbara K., *Protestant Poetics and the Seventeenth Century Religious Lyric*, Princeton, Princeton University Press, 1979.

A comprehensive study of generic theory derived from the Bible, of significance beyond the specific period to which it addresses itself.

Lewis, C. Day, *The Lyric Impulse*, London, Chatto & Windus, 1965.

MacLean, Norman, 'From action to image: theories of the lyric in the eighteenth century', in *Critics and Criticism*, ed. R. S. Crane, Chicago, Chicago University Press, 1952.

Usefully complements Abrams's work, and brings together many interesting contemporary comments on the lyric.

Welsh, Andrew, *Roots of Lyric*, Princeton, Princeton University Press, 1978.

Wide-ranging and stimulating exploration.

Form and metre

Attridge, Derek, *The Rhythms of English Poetry*, London, Longman, 1982.

Outstandingly the best study of the subject, and with a very comprehensive bibliography.

Fussell, Paul, *Poetic Meter and Poetic Form*, New York, Random House, 1979.

Traditional terminology, but some useful material.

Hollander, John, *Rhyme's Reason*, New Haven and London, Yale University Press, 1981.

A witty modern version of Pope's 'An Essay on Criticism'.

Leech, Geoffrey N., *A Linguistic Guide to English Poetry*, London, Longman, 1969.

Skelton, Robin, *The Practice of Poetry*, London, Heinemann, 1971.

Some sound commonsense observations.

Smith, Barbara H., *Poetic Closure*, Chicago, Chicago University Press, 1968.

Another very fine book, which well repays serious study. Its implications extend far beyond its stated subject, 'How poems end'.

Music and lyric

Booth, Mark W., *The Experience of Songs*, New Haven and London, Yale University Press, 1981.

Fascinating studies largely of popular and therefore neglected lyrics and music.

Hollander, John, *The Untuning of the Sky*, Princeton, Princeton University Press, 1961.

A detailed study of the neo-Platonic view of the symbolic relationship between the arts.

Ing, Catherine, *Elizabethan Lyrics*, London, Chatto & Windus, 1951.

Jurgens, Elise B., *Let Well Tun'd Words Amaze*, Minneapolis, Iowa University Press, 1981.

Principally about verse and song in the seventeenth century.

Le Huray, Peter, and Day, James (eds), *Music and Aesthetics in the Eighteenth and Early Nineteenth Centuries*, Cambridge, Cambridge University Press, 1981.

A fine collection of material, much of it bearing on the relationship between words and music.

Lindley, David, *Thomas Campion*, Leiden, E. J. Brill (forthcoming).

Devotes a chapter to this subject.

Pattison, Bruce, *Music and Poetry of the English Renaissance*, 2nd edn, London, Methuen, 1970.

Still a standard work, though getting rather out-of-date.

Stevens, John, *Music and Poetry in the Early Tudor Court*, London, Methuen, 1961.

Still one of the best joint studies, especially for its sense of the social and public dimension of sung lyric.

Winn, James Anderson, *Unsuspected Eloquence*, New Haven and London, Yale University Press, 1981.

A comprehensive survey of the relationship between the two arts from classical times to the present.

Index